21st Century

Seven Words for the 21st Century

Edited by
Edmund Newell

with an introduction by
Richard Harries

DARTON · LONGMAN + TODD

The seven last words are best known in traditional language. For this reason all references to them are from the Revised Standard Version. All other biblical references and quotations are taken from the New Revised Standard Version.

First published in 2002 by
Darton, Longman and Todd Ltd
1 Spencer Court
140–142 Wandsworth High Street
London SW18 4JJ

ISBN 0–232–52469–6

A catalogue record for this book is available from the British Library.

Designed by Sandie Boccacci
Phototypeset in 12/14.5pt Joanna
By Intype London Limited
Printed and bound in Great Britain by
The Cromwell Press, Trowbridge, Wiltshire

Contents

Preface

The idea for this book and CD came after a casual remark by a vicar on Good Friday 1998 that I might like to lead the Three Hours' Devotion at his church the following year. Perhaps the thought slipped or he changed his mind, but for whatever reason the invitation never arrived. His suggestion did, however, make me think about how I would tackle such a challenging service. To deliver something that can hold people's attention for this time and do justice to such a profoundly important occasion in the Christian calendar is a daunting prospect. As I explored various possibilities, the theme of the seven last words had particular appeal as it offers scope not only to reflect on Christ's sufferings, but it also provides an opportunity to consider how these words and the events of Good Friday speak to the contemporary Church and society. It seemed to me that this dual approach of inward reflection and outward expression is precisely what meditation should be about.

Then shortly before Christmas that year I discussed my thoughts with a friend (and fellow contributor) on a walk on Boars Hill, over-looking Oxford. Perhaps it was the combination of that famous view of the 'dreaming spires' and the spark of our discussion that led to the idea of a book and of asking people whom I had known during my time in Oxford to reflect on how the seven last words spoke to them. After all, we are accustomed to hearing the passion narratives from the differing perspectives of the four evangelists, and it seemed to us that a group of writers who could work synergistically would produce something more creative and insightful than the thoughts of a single person. And so authors were approached, and drafts were written, shared and commented on both at a workshop in the Crypt of St Paul's Cathedral and in that more recent meeting-place, cyberspace.

Meditating on the seven last words is greatly enriched by the use of music, and it became obvious that such a project would be incomplete without it. The range of music written for the seven last words is considerable, but given the contemporary nature of the project, it seemed right to look to the work of a contemporary composer. The music of Adrian Snell, which effortlessly bridges popular and classical styles, has a depth and an emotional intensity that seems right for a Good Friday meditation, and so I was delighted by Adrian's enthusiastic response to the suggestion of using his music.

This project has taken a long time to come to fruition, and so I am greatly indebted to my fellow contributors, and to Katie Worrall and Kathy Dyke at Darton, Longman and Todd, and Alex Verlek at Serious Music, not only for their creative and professional input, but also for their patience and commitment. I would like to thank Sabina Alkire who, as well as being a contributor, helped develop the idea of this book and CD. Similarly, Richard Harries offered invaluable advice in the early stages. I am also grateful to the late Bishop John Taylor, who shared his insights and his research into the background of the seven last words, and to Susan Kenny, who gave permission to use a detail from *Jesus Dies on the Cross*, by her late husband, Michael Kenny RA, as the artwork on the book-cover and CD. Many others – far too numerous to mention by name – have commented on individual chapters, and so I thank them on behalf of all the authors.

Both Adrian and I are deeply grateful to Hannah Alkire for her beautiful cello playing, and to Joe Scott for making possible a CD recorded on both sides of the Atlantic. My wife, Susan, has had to live with this project for several years. Her support, proof-reading skills and critical comments have been invaluable. Finally, I would like to thank that anonymous vicar whose remark started the process – he will be the first recipient of a complimentary book and CD, much to his surprise!

EDMUND NEWELL
St Paul's Cathedral, April 2002

List of contributors

Words

Sabina Alkire is an economist working with the United Nations, and a Non Stipendiary Minister at St Alban's and St Philip the Evangelist Churches, Washington, DC.

Helen Cunliffe is Canon Pastor of Southwark Cathedral.

Peter Doll is Team Vicar of St Michael and All Angels and St Nicolas, Abingdon.

Giles Fraser is Vicar of Putney and a Lecturer in Philosophy at Wadham College, Oxford.

Richard Harries is Bishop of Oxford.

Edmund Newell is a Canon of St Paul's Cathedral.

Tarjei Park is Vicar of Golders Green.

Hugh White is Vicar of Deddington with Barford, Clifton and Hempton.

Rowan Williams is the Archbishop of Canterbury.

Music

Adrian Snell's career as a composer, songwriter, performer and recording artist spans twenty-six years. He has recorded six major concept works and thirteen solo albums, and has performed worldwide, with many television and radio appearances to his credit.

Introduction

RICHARD HARRIES

Towards the end of the fourth century a pilgrim by the name of Egeria or Etheria, thought to be a Spanish nun, visited the Holy Land. An astute observer, Egeria recorded in a travelogue details of the many sites she visited, people she met, and acts of Christian worship she attended. Included in her *Travels* is an account of a devotional service held in Jerusalem on the Friday of the 'Great Week', the day known to us now as Good Friday. She mentions that during the service the 'holy Wood of the Cross' was on display and venerated (and kept under the protection of the bishop and deacons because someone once bit off a piece and ran away with it!). She then describes that for three hours from noon – the hours that Christ is believed to have hung on the cross – there was a service of readings on the theme of Christ's passion, interspersed with prayers and hymns. Egeria's account is the first reference to a devotional service of this kind.[1]

Sixteen hundred years later, the Three Hours' Devotion is the most popular of the Good Friday services. It is often based around a series of meditations on the 'seven last words' – those phrases recorded in the Gospels as being uttered by Christ as he hung on the cross:

'Father, forgive them; for they know not what they do.'
(Luke 23:34)

'Truly, I say to you, today you will be with me in Paradise.
(Luke 23:43)

'Woman, behold, your son! . . . Behold, your mother!'
(John 19:26f)

'Eli, Eli, lama sabachthani? . . . My God, my God, why hast thou for-saken me?' (Matt. 27:46)

'I thirst.' (John 19:28)

'It is finished.' (John 19:30)

'Father, into thy hands I commit my spirit!' (Luke 23:46)

The three hours from noon lend themselves to a period of prayer and reflection, as the worshipper symbolically joins Mary, John and the other followers of Jesus waiting at the foot of the cross. The seven last words provide a helpful structure for this, drawing the worshipper into Christ's suffering and the tumultuous events of Good Friday.

The seven last words have long been used as a set of passages for reflecting on Christ's passion. The earliest collective reference to the seven last words occurs in an eighth-century prayer of the Venerable Bede, which contrasts them with the seven deadly sins. However, it was probably not until the late seventeenth century that they came to be used in the context of a devotional service. The introduction of such a service is attributed to a Peruvian Jesuit priest, Fr Alonso Messia Bedoya, in Lima sometime after 1687. Whether or not Messia's service was original is uncertain, as there is a reference to something similar conducted by a Franciscan priest in the earlier part of the century. Nevertheless, it was Messia's version that was published and became widely adopted in Latin America and Europe.

A significant moment in the history of the seven last words was the introduction of Messia's service into the devotions of a group of pious Catholics in Cadiz, Spain, sometime in the 1760s. This group, known as the Fraternity of the Ancient Mother, met regularly to meditate on Christ's passion in a cave under the Chapel of the Rosary, known as Santa Cueva (Holy Cave). The Fraternity came under the spiritual direc-tion of a wealthy priest, Don Pedro Saenz de Santa Maria, who intro-duced Messia's service and had a grand oratory built on Santa Cueva. The significance of this is that in the 1780s the composer Joseph Haydn was commissioned to write a piece of music based on the seven last words for use in Cadiz. It is speculated that this was in connection with the blessing of the Santa Cueva oratory in 1783, although this does not tally with Haydn's own account of events. In 1801 he wrote:

It was about fifteen years ago, that I was asked by one of the Canons of Cadiz to compose a piece of instrumental music on the Seven Words of Jesus on the Cross. At that time it was the custom every year during Lent to perform an Oratorio in the Cathedral at Cadiz, the effect of which was greatly heightened by the *mise-en-scène*.

. The walls, windows and pillars of the church were draped in black cloth, and the religious gloom was lightened by one large lamp hanging in the centre. At mid-day all the doors were closed, and the music commenced. After a fitting prelude, the Bishop ascended the pulpit, recited one of the Seven Words, and gave a meditation on it. When it was ended, he came down from the pulpit and knelt before the altar. The interlude was filled with music. The Bishop mounted and left the pulpit for a second time, a third time, and so on, and on each occasion, after the close of the address, the orchestra recommenced playing.[2]

Whether or not there is a direct link between Haydn's *Seven Last Words* and Santa Cueva, what is significant is the introduction to Cadiz of the service based on the seven last words, as it led to the commissioning of the music by Haydn. Haydn's *Seven Last Words* quickly became one of his most popular works – with the original orchestral version later scored for both string quartet and quintet, which allowed it to be performed more easily and more widely, as well as for choir.

One interesting feature of Haydn's composition is that after the seventh word there is a final adagio, 'Il Terremoto' ('The Earthquake'). This refers to the earthquake at the moment of Christ's death recorded in Matthew 27:50–51. However, this section may also provide an important clue as to why Messia's service became popular in Europe in the latter part of the eighteenth century. This is because Messia is thought to have conceived the service in response to a devastating earthquake in Peru in 1687. At the time, this natural disaster was believed by many to be an act of divine retribution for the sins of the people of Peru, and so it is suggested that Messia initially held the service as an act of penitence on behalf of those who survived the earthquake. Messia's opening meditation would certainly resonate with penitent victims of an earthquake:

All nature is disturbed at beholding the suffering of its Creator. The earth is covered with a thick darkness; an earthquake rends the rocks asunder, and bursts open the graves; the angels are horror-stricken at beholding their Lord in such cruel torments; the devils rage with anger, because the chastisement which men deserve for their sins is not immediately inflicted on them, as it was upon themselves.[3]

The European connection occurs because in 1755 a serious earthquake affected much of Portugal and Spain. The Lisbon earthquake of 1 November took place at 9.30 a.m. on a Sunday morning when many were attending church, and among the thousands of victims were large numbers of worshippers. This earthquake had a profound effect on the people of Europe, and particularly upon the churches, which sought to come to terms with the circumstances of the devastation. Although Lisbon was worst affected, the earthquake's impact was widespread, and the port of Cadiz was struck by a 60-foot tidal wave. Against this background, it is highly plausible that Messia's service would have found a place in the worship of a generation that bore the physical and psychological scars of an earthquake and who sought to make sense of this 'act of God'.

Whatever the reason for its introduction in Europe, the service rapidly gained popularity. Soon those conducting the service produced their own addresses, and the success of Haydn's music led to a different format to that devised by Messia being widely adopted. In Messia's original format each address was followed by silence, the recitation of appropriate verses, and prayers. In the new format, following Haydn's example, each address was followed by music. It is this combination of word and music that has proved popular and has been widely used ever since, both in devotional services and concert performances.

Haydn was not the first composer to find inspiration from the seven last words. In the 1640s the German composer Schütz wrote an oratorio on this theme, although this is more akin to a conventional passion than a set of reflective pieces. Similarly, the seven last words feature in Graun's *The Death of Jesus* (1755). Like Schütz and Graun, many composers have reflected on the seven last words within oratorios or works based on Christ's passion, including Beethoven, Spohr, Williams,

Gounod, Stainer, Somervell, and Mercandante. Others have followed more closely Haydn's format, including Dubois, Cesar Franck, Tournemire, Gubaidulina and, most recently, James MacMillan and Ian Wilson, while a recording by American rock musicians, *At the Foot of the Cross*, offers a strikingly different interpretation. Such a long history and wide variety of styles indicates what an enduring and inspiring theme the seven last words have proved to be.

As well as music, numerous books of meditations on the seven last words have been published – the British Library catalogue currently lists well over a hundred. The theme has a widespread appeal across Christian denominations and traditions. Within Catholicism, entering Christ's suffering has long been regarded as a means of gaining spiritual insight into what it means to 'take up your cross and follow me'. From a Protestant perspective, the cross is revered as the means by which Christ redeemed humanity. It is perhaps for these reasons that the Good Friday Three Hours' Devotion has its roots in Catholicism, but has become widespread amongst Protestant churches. Within the Anglican Church, its first use was probably by the Victorian ritualist the Revd A. H. Mackonochie, at St Alban's, Holborn, London, in 1864. The service soon became popular, and an account of the service at St Paul's, Knightsbridge, in 1869, reported that 'Hard-headed men of business, Members of Parliament, and many of both sexes, who are better known in the world of fashion than in the assembly of the sanctuary – were there.'[4] The first English cathedral to adopt the service was St Paul's in 1878.

The seven last words also appear from time to time in other forms of literature. John Donne's final sermon, delivered in 1630, draws a parallel between the seven last words and the seven days of the week. Gerard Manley Hopkins' seven 'terrible' sonnets are based on the seven last words. The seven last words appear in James Joyce's *Ulysses*, while in his *Stephen Hero* (an early version of *A Portrait of the Artist as a Young Man*), the main character attends a Three Hour Devotion, after which he agonises over the seven last words. Dylan Thomas' poem 'Altarwise by Owl-light' paraphrases the seven last words, Samuel Beckett alludes to them in his play *Waiting for Godot*, as does Ted Hughes in 'The Seven Sorrows'. Such uses of, and references to, the seven last words indicate the profundity and emotional depth of these short phrases.

This book and CD draws on the Haydn format of Good Friday meditations of word and music. But rather than using the seven last words to focus inwards on Christ's suffering, together they offer a strikingly different and contemporary approach. The book begins with a chapter by Rowan Williams on the meaning of the cross in contemporary society, and subsequent chapters take each of the seven last words as the starting-point to develop a thought-provoking and challenging reflection, drawing on insights from theology, history, literature, ethics, film criticism, and economics – offering insights into how the seven words can speak afresh in the early years of the twenty-first century. Each chapter ends with a short meditation, which relates to a track on the CD. The music has been carefully selected to reflect the meaning and mood of each meditation, drawing on Adrian Snell's extensive repertoire in which he has explored the passion of Christ, the human condition and the Jewish roots of Christianity. After reading each chapter, readers are invited to reflect on what they have read, using both the meditation and the music.

I first heard a three-hour meditation based on the seven last words as an ordinand at Cuddesdon in the early 1960s. I found the preacher oppressive and, in order to maintain my equilibrium, let alone my faith, I slipped out and disappeared to the bottom of a nearby field to read Paul Tillich's *The Courage to Be*. This book, with its encouraging message that even in the most radical act of doubt there is an affirmation of faith, saved the day for me.

When I was a young curate in Hampstead the three hours was an altogether different experience. It was delivered every year by the Revd Joseph McCulloch, the Rector of Mary-le-Bow, in the parish of Hampstead. People came from all over London and virtually everyone stayed for the whole three hours. Always relating the seven last words to some other theme, such as Shakespeare's seven ages of man, the addresses were both enthralling and profound. We all came out feeling we had entered more deeply into the mystery both of Jesus and our own lives.

Having delivered Good Friday addresses a good number of times in the course of my own ministry, there are two significant changes from those days. First, far more churches have a liturgy on Good Friday as well as addresses, so the actual time to meditate on the seven last words may be shorter. Secondly, as a result of biblical scholarship, it is important and more helpful to draw out, through the words, the different insights of each evangelist. In short, rather than seeing the seven last words as a composite whole, it is good to stress the distinctive perspectives of the different evangelists.

I commend this book and CD most warmly for use in personal meditation by individual Christians and as a source of inspiration for those who have to speak on Good Friday. As it happens, the authors all have a connection with both the University and the Diocese of Oxford. In addition to Rowan Williams, formerly a Professor in the University and a Canon of Christ Church Cathedral, whose writings are appreciated round the world, there is an interesting mixture of younger theologians with fresh insights to share. Sabina Alkire and Edmund Newell, for example, were both academic economists before turning to theology. Hugh White is a distinguished scholar of English literature. But over and above their academic backgrounds there is a strong shared desire, as the title of the book and CD makes plain, to show how the seven last words which the evangelists report as having been uttered by Jesus on the cross, relate to the concerns of the present century. The Welsh priest and poet R. S. Thomas once said in a BBC programme:

> I think I am content to say I am a Christian because I think Christianity, the Christian doctrine, is the most profound and satisfactory answer to the great problem of suffering. [I don't think] even in this late stage of the 20th century there is anything more contemporary than the cross.[5]

The insights of these chapters, together with the accompanying music, will bear out the truth of that remark.

The cross in the 21st century

ROWAN WILLIAMS

When Jesus of Nazareth was crucified, crosses were a daily sight. They reminded people who was in charge in Roman Palestine, what the cost was of offering any kind of challenge to the occupying power. When Jesus had encouraged his disciples to pick up their crosses and follow him, he was speaking with a kind of grim irony: if you're going to follow me, you should know that, one way or another, it's an act of rebellion, an act that will, one way or another, cost you your life. It was a live metaphor because it was so immediate a reality.

In the nearly two thousand years that have passed, language about crosses has become dead metaphor. The cross now lives only in religious language – whereas in the first century it represented things that were as far as you could imagine from religion. As Paul points out, the connection between crucifixion and God was shocking, tasteless and uncomfortable for Jews and non-Jews alike. But in a world where crosses are mainly seen in churches or around people's necks, what has happened to the original, difficult, transformative content of the language? How can the cross be talked about now in a way that makes a difference?

'Take up your cross' now means, 'Put up with your minor discomforts', or, at most, 'Be sure that you do something to show God that you take him seriously by making yourself uncomfortable in some way.' 'We all have our crosses to bear' means that we must all demonstrate perseverance in circumstances we don't fully control. The cross is as much a daily sight as it was in Jesus' day, but for a quite different reason: it has become a sign for something disconnected from the actual experiences of power and powerlessness, fear and hope, in society; it has become the marker of a minority interest group, who seem to use it with rather obsessional frequency. If Jesus' Palestine was full of crosses, so is many a church; but the difference is plain.

It isn't an answer to this if we simply intensify the emotional charge of the religious symbol by stressing the extremity of the suffering depicted. That has been done pretty regularly since the late Middle Ages; it is still done by contemporary artists who are determined to shock. The truth is that we can find plenty of examples of extreme suffering (and people always have been able to find them), many of them more immediately effective for us than the image of the crucified. And once we acknowledge that what we are looking for is just images of suffering, we might well ask a few questions about our motivation. The rather murky psychological background to some of the Christian fascination with the cross is hard to evade. Paul knew that the shock of the cross was not how badly Jesus suffered. (What about those who lingered on the cross for days? What about the other ways in which a law-abiding empire tortured its non-citizens to death?) We need, in thinking about the cross, to move beyond the attempt to bring emotions to the boil by pretending that this was, by definition, a uniquely awful form of physical pain.

There are two things we probably ought to hold in our minds if we want to understand afresh what meditation on the cross is properly for. The first is what we have already noted: in its context, the proclamation of God's involvement in the cross says something about power and risk. The second is to do with what makes this cross, among all the others in its era, significant, world-changingly significant.

To walk with Jesus and to belong with the God of Jesus is risky; but not in the simple sense that you might become a martyr for the divine cause. That's bearable, even attractive to a certain mind-set. We hardly need reminding of that in today's world of suicide bombers. The majority of those crucified in Roman Judea and Galilee were not in fact modern freedom fighters but a mixture of petty thugs, delinquent or runaway slaves and innocents executed for the purposes of plain state terror. The crucified is literally nailed up as a notice of what the powerful mean to say; the crucified is not a martyr but more of a cypher, a naked and more or less anonymous signifier in the language of someone else (the governing authority). The cross is not about extremity of suffering so much as extremity of helplessness, impotence in speaking what you mean to say.

To walk with Jesus and the God of Jesus, then, is to risk having nothing to say that power can hear, to risk becoming a cypher in someone else's scheme of things. This is why it is not just politically-correct sentimentality to imagine the meaning of the cross in relation to the experience of a raped woman or an abused child. Again and again we are told that the anguish here is so often that of being deprived of any way of describing what has happened except in terms of the story told by the possessor of power: the woman or the child is pre-emptively seen as the one who provokes desire and so shares responsibility for the act which invades and silences them.

The cross is where the non-citizens are executed; it defines the fact, much thought about by the earliest Christians, that belonging with the God of Jesus is the opposite of being a citizen, someone with clear, publicly agreed rights and status. The 'rights' of the Christian are grounded in active relation with God and each other rather than the law of the state. And this is not simply a transition into a mildly utopian community alongside the state (as if coming to belong with Jesus were like joining CND or the Green Party); it is to invite the unwelcome fate of being written out of the story, having no meaning that the public sphere can grasp. This has nothing to do with any kind of commendation by the powerful to the powerless to accept their doubtless disagreeable lot. It is an observation that in a society where non-citizens can be painfully and fairly casually slaughtered, God is not a citizen; so that if we are to be found where God is, we can't stay safely within our citizen's rights.

So recovering the sense of what the cross is about involves us first in some reflection on becoming a non-citizen alongside God. The cross is a gateway into that strange community in which non-citizens belong together because they belong with God. God in the cross accepts the fate of being silenced, deprived of the words to utter his own meaning. But this is not to say that God expects us to be silenced by the murderous injustice of the world. To be unequivocally with him is to be stripped of the ordinary ways of making sense, stripped of what might carry weight in the world's frame of reference. But to be with him is also to be with all who are, by their choice or the choice of others, non-citizens, non-belongers; it is to be part of a social order that depends on nothing but God's presence and self-gift, God's decision to be with the non-belongers. It is this vision that makes the writer of the Letter to the Hebrews encourage believers to go to where Jesus is 'outside the camp', looking for a 'city' that doesn't yet exist (13:13–14). And looking for a non-existent city is rather more than accepting passively a situation of oppression; it is to be involved in building and sustaining alternatives to the way the world makes sense.

Following Jesus leads to where God is; following Jesus leads to places where people are robbed of their speech and their social power. God is to be discovered where social power runs out, as the reality that has nothing in common with social power. Only with this in mind can we grasp how the cross begins to be the act of creating a new communal phenomenon, sufficiently new and peculiar to be still, two thousand years on, tantalisingly hard to describe and constantly trying to evade its own distinctiveness. The cross is where Christian distinctiveness is focused – not because Christianity is first and foremost a religion of suffering, but because it is a social reality constituted by the strange impact of divine action in the death of someone by this particular method which is associated with the slave and the non-citizen.

But all this relates to the second theme mentioned, the question of what makes this crucifixion different and decisive. The answer is already there in essence. This is the crucifixion of someone who claims to speak for God. To follow him, he has said, is to be with God; his words and actions, he says or implies, are a renewal of God's call to God's people, widening out the definition of who may be part of God's people with a startling disregard for the conventional interpretation of acceptable criteria for this. He promises being with God and his path leads to the cross; so that we are starkly challenged as to whether we can cope with identifying this place of execution as God's place.

In the light of Jesus' words and actions, the crucifixion is the drastic rejection of God's action, God's call. What is crucified is the embodi-ment of divine promise or grace, which is nailed up as superfluous, threatening, empty and lethally dangerous all at once by those who cannot hear what promise means. It is true to say that God is crucified. And once again, we should be cautious about turning this simply into a drama of suffering – the transcendent God at last experiencing human woe, rather like a King Lear deprived of his royalty and 'feeling what wretches feel'. This has a certain emotional force, but it can also be a sentimental projection. What is done on the cross is not about the intensity with which God feels human sorrow (a coherent doctrine of God ought to have told us already that the God of the First Covenant knows precisely what human grief and loss are; if he needs to become incarnate to know it, something odd is being said about both the nature of God and the Hebrew Scriptures). It is about where God *is*; and about what human hatred and self-hatred actually means.

The rejection of Jesus is the rejection of an unconditional promise of God's fellowship. And this is not simply saying no to a potentially attractive but finally optional human good; if human beings are made in God's likeness and designed to share the divine life in some sense, the rejection of Jesus is the rejection of humanity itself by humanity. The cross is the human imagination cutting off the branch it is sitting on, trying to pull up its own roots. And so we can make some further connections. To stand with God is to stand with those who don't belong; but those who don't belong may be found on the cross, dying the death of a slave. God is the author of the invitation to life itself, and more specifically of the invitation to life in the company of Jesus as the one who assures us concretely and historically of our divine welcome; God creates a kind of belonging without analogues in the 'natural' world. And so to refuse to stand where Jesus is is to push against the very grain of creation, to deny what I am created to be, to decline to belong with God. Yet God has chosen to belong with us; and if we refuse to belong with him, he is still to be found with us in our self-rejection or self-exclusion, since he cannot define his position as another sort of 'ordinary' belonging with its conditions and limitations.

The crucified Jesus is not only the God who stands with the non-citizen; he also tells me that my refusals of his invitation are self-destructive – and that therefore the way I desire to keep at a distance from those who don't belong is a self-deprivation, ultimately a self-refusal.

Here it is in the lines of Charles Causley's poem, 'I Am the Great Sun. From a Normandy crucifix of 1632':

> I am the great sun, but you do not see me,
> I am your husband, but you turn away . . .
> I am your counsel, but you do not hear me,
> I am the lover whom you will betray,
> I am the victor, but you do not cheer me,
> I am the holy dove whom you will slay.
> I am your life, but if you will not name me,
> Seal up your soul with tears, and never blame me.[1]

Reflecting on the cross in the contemporary world is, I've been suggesting, more than just thinking about the inescapable realities of tragedy or about God's involvement with suffering. It is the painful process of taking up a stance, 'staking yourself' in Gillian Rose's favoured phrase. Understood as the distinctive word of an active God, the cross invites us to ask where we stand, with whom; and to ask what we have done to ourselves in the whole human record of mutual refusal and rejection. We are confronted with the fact of God's stance, God's self-staking, in such a way that we cannot escape the conclusion that the violence of human refusal is suicidal. The death I collude with, the death and silencing of the one with no rights, no citizenship, is my death because it is God's death, the death God has chosen to make his own so as to speak to us and act for us and upon us.

From the very first, believers have seen the cross as an action, not only a passion, something done, not only the record of things done to someone. Hence the cry of triumph, 'It is finished', at the climax of St John's story of the crucifixion. The cross is the end of Jesus' journey in the name and power of God to where people are deprived of humanity – by suffering oppression, by being silenced, but also by their own fear and withdrawal. It completes the picture of how God's transforming love works by showing us where that love can be seen. It is the sign and the substance of God's decision to be where his human creation tries hardest to kill itself. At precisely the point where we exercise most energy and ingenuity in attempting to dig up our roots in God's creative love, that love reasserts itself.

Hence it makes sense to speak of the cross as the paying of a price:

the bearer of God's life bears the consequence of human self-hatred, the cost of human fear. What is unique on the cross of Jesus is not either some special intensity of agony or some abstract transaction to placate God's justice. It is the fact that this death, this slave's death, is carried by the one who has consistently and unbrokenly carried God's absolute promise in his every act and word. As in the Gospel of John, it is as if people were being invited to express their fear and hatred in unprecedentedly direct form: here is the mercy of God; this is what you hate and fear when you hate and fear each other. And by bearing this in God's name and power, the cross creates a different kind of citizenship by its invitation to belong with the God of non-belongers.

So we reflect on the words from the cross in the light of this central word: here is where God has chosen to be. Here is where the barriers are broken down between God and the darkest places of the human mind; and so here too is where the barriers are down between human beings. The death of Jesus on the cross marks the creation of an unbreakable alliance, a covenant, between God and humanity, made visible in the covenant community: entering the community is by choosing to be where Christ is in his death (baptism), participation is bound up with eating and drinking together in the faith that the common nourishment of bread and wine is in fact nourishment with the life that on the cross expressed the desire of God to be in the world like this.

Here is where God has chosen to be. But this is not a matter of human imagination recognising God through this shocking event by some great leap of intuitive perception. Christians have understood the resurrection as God's 'indication' of his presence on the cross. The resurrection is God displaying the crucified body to us, saying that here in this wounded body is still where he lives and speaks. It is so often remarked that the risen Jesus in the Gospels does not appear as a glorified and resplendent body but as the one who – visibly – has suffered death. He is recognised by his wounds. What is being said is not only that God's love is undefeated by human rejection, but that this love continues to embody itself exactly as in Jesus' ministry – that ministry which leads inexorably to the slave's death. There is no way around or behind the 'form of the slave' to a smoother or calmer version of what divine love means, no way of internalising that love into our own feelings of comfort and acceptance. The divine love made flesh continues to be the love that is visible on the cross of the non-citizen, with all that means for our own conversion and incorporation into the community of the non-citizens.

The resurrection 'displays' the cross – but not as an ideal or an abstract summons to individual faith. It displays the body of the crucified as alive, and as (in the way it was before) the concrete place of God's call to reconciliation with God and each other. To pick up Paul's imagery, the crucified body is the throne in the Holy of Holies, the *kapporeth* where atonement is made. But it is in the light of the resurrection that this can be seen and said, because the resurrection is the manifesting of the fact that God *continues* to choose to be where the crucified Jesus is, and thus makes the crucified Jesus alive as body, as person.

Reflecting on the cross does not, for the believer, simply begin with the cross as an historical event; it begins from recognising – as a result of God's act in the resurrection – what is unique in this cross as well as what in the cross is the universal truth of our untruthful humanity. It begins with recognising that this is the place where God and humanity are displayed in equal clarity and fullness. It is the ultimately irreligious place; and at the same time the Holy of Holies. It changes what holiness means because it changes our estimate of where God is. And if we are serious about it, it changes not simply what we think or feel, but literally where we are, where we find ourselves.

SO WHERE AM I?

I'm terrified of finding myself there because I can't cope with not being able to make sense. I want to be talking the same language as others. After all, how shall I witness to God if I'm talking in terms no one understands?

I know that I'm supposed to believe that this is where God chooses to be, but I don't believe it. God is full of compassion for the lost, the non-belongers, the non-citizens, but he's still God, after all, and he must surely want me to be who I am in effective and sensible ways, so that I can point people to his transcendence.

And all he will say to me is, 'Here is your life, and nowhere else.' He says, 'I don't ask you first to be effective and eloquent; first I ask you to be where I am and to be alive. You can spend all the years of your life struggling to be an effective witness for me, but if you haven't been here with me you are not yet alive.'

It looks as though what I hate is the thought of being alive; just being where he is, irrespective of what I have done or can do or have said or can say. And I hate the thought of being alive only with, only alongside, those who have turned their backs on success or who have already 'lost' in whatever battles there are to be fought.

I don't know if I can cope with there being no battles to win, with God having already dissolved that whole frame of reference. And I'm not sure I want life that can only be lived in such company.

I die because I will not die. I seal up my soul with tears because I will not take the step to where God is and join God's company, so long as the cost is what it is.

And I'm not even sure what the first step might be to where God is.

Perhaps if I could just see the nearest and most obvious non-citizen in whom God calls to me; if I could just see where the boundaries are that I must cross here and now . . .

I want to see because I do want life. No I don't, I want it on my solitary terms. Yes I do, because I see how people die like that. I'm at war with myself; who will deliver me from this body condemned to die?

I want and I don't want; I see and I don't see. Give me time, God, give me strength to want with the centre of myself. Give me room in my heart for the truth I think I hate and know I love.

2

'Father, forgive them; for they know not what they do' (Luke 23:34)

EDMUND NEWELL

Curiously, these first of the seven last words are omitted from some of the earliest manuscripts of Luke's Gospel. Why should this be so? Why should those who carefully transcribed the text remove from the lips of the dying Christ this prayer for forgiveness? Could it be a mistake, or was it deliberate?

It is unlikely to have been an error. To omit accidentally such a profound statement by Christ at a climactic moment in the Gospel seems implausible. And yet it seems equally implausible that Christ's compassionate prayer for forgiveness should be erased deliberately – unless we allow for the chilling possibility that those who transcribed the Gospel believed that the people for whom Jesus prayed were beyond forgiveness.

Or could we be looking at this the wrong way round? Is it possible that rather than being removed, these words – which are unique to Luke's Gospel – were instead added to the original version, to indicate that those who were held responsible for Christ's crucifixion should be forgiven for their actions? There is no consensus amongst biblical scholars as to which, if either, interpretation is correct. But the puzzle does beg a further question: who was it that the evangelist or later editor believed Jesus prayed for?

We might reasonably assume that the prayer refers to the Roman soldiers. After all, they were acting under orders to crucify a convicted criminal, presumably oblivious to the religious complexities of the situation. But in Luke's account of events it is not the Romans who are held accountable for Christ's crucifixion, it is 'the Jews' – both the religious leaders and the crowd. After Pilate passes sentence he hands Jesus 'over as they [the Jews] wished' (23:25). The narrative continues in a way that implies that 'they' (the Jews) are responsible for what follows. And so when Jesus prays, 'Father, forgive them; for they know not what they do', there can be little doubt that the 'they' he refers to are also 'the Jews'.

The clinching argument for this interpretation is found not in Luke's Gospel, but in the Acts of the Apostles, the companion volume to the Gospel. There is a clear and deliberate parallel between Jesus' prayer for forgiveness and the prayer uttered by Stephen as he was stoned to death by Jewish executioners: 'Lord, do not hold this sin against them' (Acts 7:60). Stephen, the first Christian martyr, is portrayed as following Christ on the way of the cross, to the point of echoing his Lord's compassionate plea on behalf of his killers at the time of his own death.

The evidence points to the conclusion that those who transcribed Luke's Gospel either deliberately omitted Christ's prayer of forgiveness because of strong anti-Jewish feelings, or added it to counter hostility towards the Jews, linking it with Stephen's prayer. Both explanations make sense given what's known of Christian–Jewish relations at the time.

The sad truth is that as Christianity broke away from its Jewish roots in the late first and second centuries, considerable hostility was shown by some Christians towards Jews, and by some Jews towards Christians. As the predominantly Gentile Christian Church began to develop its own distinct identity, a bitter hatred towards the Jewish people surfaced within certain quarters. From what began as sibling rivalry between faith communities that shared much in common but disagreed on some significant issues, something much more sinister emerged. Anti-Judaism among Christians fed on the negativity towards Jews that had long existed in the Roman and Greek worlds but took it much further, theologising and institutionalising it within the Church. Thus began a troubled history of relations between Christians and Jews that has lasted for centuries and that has only relatively recently begun to be healed. And even today, there is still much to be done to counter the anti-Judaism that persists subconsciously within Christianity.

When people are exposed for the first time to the history of anti-Judaism within the Church they are shocked – as indeed the author of this chapter was shocked – as it seems so much at odds with the Christian ethic of loving one's neighbour. What's more, it soon becomes apparent that the heritage of the Church's teaching and actions over the centuries may well have helped create the conditions that made the Holocaust possible. This, too, is a shocking realisation. And yet without exposure to this history it's all too easy not to see the destructiveness of so much that was said and done in the name of Christ, and to perpetuate the prejudices which have been the cause of so much pain and misery to so many people for nearly 2,000 years. For this reason alone it is important that this unsavoury aspect of the Church's history should not be brushed aside.

But there is another pressing reason to reflect on the past. Exposure to the troubled history of Christian–Jewish relations also raises our awareness of the potential destructiveness of other expressions of religious intolerance so prevalent in our world, particularly the hostility shown towards those who are differentiated from others – or us – by their custom, practice or belief. It is then that Jesus' prayer from the cross addresses a new constituency: it is each generation through its ignorance and folly that is in need of God's forgiveness. The Christ who died for us all prays for us all.

For Christians of all denominations and traditions, Good Friday is a profoundly moving and solemn day. It calls for quiet reflection and contemplation as we enter into the mystery of Christ's suffering and death. The Three Hours' Liturgy, of which the seven last words are so often a part, heightens the intensity of the occasion as we wait at the foot of the cross, focusing on the final agonising moments of Christ's life.

On Good Friday of all days, the futility of so much human suffering inflicted at the hands of fellow human beings becomes all too apparent. It is therefore a sad irony that for many centuries Good Friday was a day of fear for Jewish people. The reason is that from a very early stage in the Church's history 'the Jews' were blamed for Christ's death, and so were often targeted for revenge attacks on the day when the crucifixion was most powerfully recollected. Such action was not merely an expression of mob hatred towards a religious and cultural minority, it was underpinned by the teaching and witness of some of the most revered theologians and leaders of the early Church, drawing on many harsh statements found in the New Testament.

The Austrian historian Friedrich Heer refers to the fourth century as 'the era in which the fires of Christian hate and murder were lit' – in some cases, quite literally. In 338 a synagogue in Callinicum in Syria was burnt down, to which event St Ambrose responded, 'I hereby declare, that it was I who set fire to the synagogue; indeed I gave orders for it to be done so that there should no longer be any place where Christ is denied.'[1]

It was also in the fourth century that what is known as the 'theology of contempt' towards Jews took hold. It was in Antioch in Syria in 387 that St John Chrysostom delivered a series of eight sermons now known as *Against the Jews*, designed to stop local Christian interest in Jewish festivals. In these sermons he reiterated forcefully a charge first made by Melito, Bishop of Sardis, in the second century, that in the crucifixion of Jesus the Jews had committed the ultimate crime of deicide – killing God. Focusing on the local synagogue and Jewish community, he wrote, 'It is time for me to show that demons dwell in the synagogue not only in the place itself, but in the souls of the Jews.'[2] St Jerome added fuel to the fire by delivering a devastating attack on the Antioch synagogue: 'If you call it a brothel, a den of vice, the Devil's refuge, Satan's fortress, a place to deprave the soul, an abyss of every conceivable disaster or whatever else you will, you are still saying less than it deserves!'[3] Even when allowance is made for the rhetorical style that was common and acceptable in another era, the invective is shock-ing. Such statements were not merely hype, they were expressions of belief by people of influence who gave anti-Judaism a firm footing in the formative years of the Christian Church.

The very idea that Jews living over 300 years after the death of Christ could in any way be held responsible for the crucifixion may seem absurd. Yet theologians had an answer, turning to a key passage in Matthew's account of the crucifixion: 'So when Pilate saw that he could do nothing, but rather that a riot was beginning, he took some water and washed his hands before the crowd, saying, "I am innocent of this man's blood; see to it yourselves." Then the people answered as a whole, "His blood be on us and on our children!"' (27:24–25). This condemnation by the Jewish crowd of themselves and of future generations – the so-called 'blood curse' – provided the evidence that the Jews were collectively culpable in Christ's death in a way akin to original sin: that all Jews are tainted with the sin of their forebears. The theologian Origen expressed this view in the third century: 'The blood of Jesus was not only on those who were present at the time, but also on every succeeding generation of Jews until the end of the World.'[4]

Christian theologians also interpreted the troubled events of Jewish history in relation to Christ's death. The destruction of Jerusalem and the Jewish Temple by the Romans in AD 70 following a Jewish revolt was seen as an act of divine punishment, as was the subsequent displacement of many Jewish people from their homeland. The 'myth of the wandering Jew' was expounded by St Eusebius in the fourth century, who described the Jewish Diaspora in these terms: 'they [the Jews] would be dispersed among the gentiles throughout the whole world, with never a hope of any cessation of evil or breathing space from troubles.'[5]

By the fifth century, the Jews were not only under attack from Church leaders, but following the adoption of Christianity as the official religion of the Roman Empire, they became subject to state sanctions. This political and social ostracism led to a further theological twist to the myth of the wandering Jew by none other than St Augustine, perhaps the most influential theologian in the Church's history. Witnessing the plight of the Jews, Augustine argued that although they deserved to die because of the crucifixion, they were instead allowed to live and suffer to serve as a witness to the truth of the Church's teaching. He described them as having 'the mark of Cain', who was spared death but sentenced by God to be rootless and to wander the earth for killing his brother Abel (Gen. 4:1–16).

Legislation introduced by the Emperor Justinian in the sixth century took the state persecution of the Jews much further. All synagogues in

Africa were confiscated and handed over to the Church, and Jews were excluded from most occupations. Similarly, Church law began to impose restrictions on Jews. One of the earliest examples is the ruling of the Third Council of Orleans in 538, which forbade Jews to appear on the street between Maundy Thursday and Easter Monday. Although this may have been in part for their own protection, it also reinforced hostile attitudes towards Jews at this sensitive time of year.

Many more instances of anti-Judaism at this time could be added to the list. But the point is clear: in the early centuries of the Church's history its dominant attitude towards the Jews was one of hostility. It did not seem to matter that Jesus was Jewish, that Mary was Jewish, that the apostles were Jewish, or that Christianity had emerged as a Jewish sect. As a former Chief Rabbi of Vienna once wrote, 'The Christian kneels before the image of the Jew, wrings his hands before the image of a Jewess; his Apostles, Festivals and Psalms are Jewish', yet Christians 'wreak vengeance upon the rest of the Jews by treating them as devils.'[6]

To catalogue the troubled history of the persecution of Jews in a few pages is an impossible task, but some notorious events stand out. After several centuries of relative calm, anti-Jewish feelings were stirred again by the religious fervour of the Crusades. As Christian soldiers moved onwards to Jerusalem to take the Holy Sepulchre from Muslim invaders in the First Crusade, they attacked Jews en route. It is estimated that in the first six months of 1096, 10,000 Jews in northern France and Germany were killed. At the end of their journey in 1099, the Crusaders burnt down the Jerusalem synagogue, which was filled with Jews.

Throughout the Middle Ages, Europe witnessed the widespread persecution and demonising of Jews. In England, the murder of a young boy near Norwich just after Easter in 1144 was blamed on Jews, leading to the allegation that Jews deliberately crucified Christian children during Holy Week to re-enact Christ's crucifixion and mock the Christian faith. This myth spread and developed into what is known as 'the blood libel', whereby Jews were accused not only of murdering Christian children, but of using their blood to make unleavened bread for the Passover celebration.

By the thirteenth century, Jews were also accused of desecrating consecrated communion hosts – and thereby defiling Christ's body. And when the Black Death swept through Europe in the fourteenth century, Jews were accused of poisoning the water in wells in order to wipe out the Christian population – an accusation which led to thousands of Jews being killed in retribution. This incident also points to another myth that has been perpetuated down the centuries: that the Jews conspire to achieve world domination. Although the Church renounced such accusations, it had nevertheless already contributed significantly towards creating an atmosphere in which they could take hold.

Also popular was the depiction of Jews as grotesque monsters in league with the devil. This image permeated art, literature and the public psyche. Such negative stereotypes were reinforced by passion plays, which became popular from the thirteenth century. As the story of the crucifixion was acted out, Jews were invariably portrayed as evil and collectively guilty for the death of Jesus. Such was the impact of these plays that they could incite mob violence. In the fifteenth century civil authorities in Europe ordered special measures to protect Jewish neighbourhoods during performances of passion plays, and in 1539 a performance in Rome had to be cancelled because in past years it had regularly led to the sacking of the Jewish quarter.

The artistic representation of Jews is no more powerfully illustrated than in the *Planctus* ('Lament of Mary') in a passion play contained in the thirteenth-century *Carmina Burana* manuscripts found in a Benedictine monastery in Bavaria:

> Oh the crimes of this hateful race,
> the animal-like hands of those crucifying you
> Oh this barbarous people
> Oh blind deplorable race!
> Oh he who is innocent is condemned by a damnable people,
> fulfilling what is necessary.
> O men of blood
> rage against the Lord of Salvation.[7]

The Middle Ages also witnessed a vast number of repressive policies imposed on Jews. In 1222 the Council of Oxford banned the building of synagogues. In 1239 Pope Gregory IX's declaration that the Talmud was heretical led to the burning of copies throughout Europe. The Council of Basel of 1434 decreed that Jews could not acquire academic degrees. A ban on land-owning and membership of trades' guilds placed considerable restrictions on occupations that Jews could practice. It led many to turn to money-lending, since the Church's ban on Christians engaging in usury (charging interest on loans) provided a rare opportunity to pursue a trade unhindered – albeit one with a stigma attached to it, as illustrated by the character of Shylock in Shakespeare's *The Merchant of Venice*.

Repressive legislation of this kind was bolstered by the thirteenth-century Church doctrine of *Servitus Judacorum* (the perpetual servitude of the Jews), which stated categorically that Jews should be subordinate to Christians. This doctrine lent support to the practice of forced conversions and baptisms of Jews, which became increasingly common, and of the widespread expulsion of Jews from countries in 'Christian' Europe. In England, Jews were expelled in 1290 and not readmitted until 1656.

The litany of intolerance and atrocities committed in the name of Jesus against his own people leads us to ask why anti-Judaism took such a firm hold in the Church. In particular, what was it that soured the mind and attitude of some of its most influential leaders, who in other respects led courageous and compassionate lives?

Perhaps part of the answer lies in the nature of traditional Jewish society. From an early date, Jews retained a very strong sense of their own religious and cultural identity when surrounded by other cultures and religions. This led to accusations of their being separatist, and their non-participation in certain social activities on religious grounds made them easy targets for persecution – a phenomenon experienced by many minority groups throughout history.

Secondly, there was a major theological issue that drove a wedge between Christians and Jews: the belief that Christianity had super-seded Judaism, and that the Church was the 'new Israel'. Indeed, there was a certain inevitability about this, given the Christian claim that Jesus was the Messiah. The Roman Catholic theologian Rosemary Ruether has even termed anti-Judaism 'the left hand of Christology', such is the sensitivity over the claim of Jesus' messianic status.[8]

And thirdly, Church leaders were strongly influenced by the anti-Jewish texts found in the New Testament – particularly in the Gospels.

In John's Gospel alone, there are about 70 references to 'the Jews' which are either negative or pejorative. For example, in a passage where Jesus is addressing 'the Jews who had believed in him', the evangelist quotes Jesus as saying, 'You are from your father the devil, and you choose to do your father's desires' (8:44). Many more instances could be added from elsewhere, such as the reference to a 'synagogue of Satan' (Rev. 2:9) and the accusation of the Jews' responsibility for the crucifixion: 'this Jesus whom you crucified' (Acts 2:36).

While some theologians have argued the contrary, there can be little doubt that such statements were intended to cast those Jews who had not adopted Christianity in a bad light. What is largely forgotten, however, is that the Gospels were written towards the end of the first century when relations between Christians and Jews were strained, and when Christianity was seeking to establish its own identity independent of its Jewish origins. It is therefore not surprising that the evangelists would reflect that tension. Neither is it surprising to find in the Jewish Talmudic writings of the same period derogatory statements about Jewish Christians, who are described as minim – separatists and heretics – or references to Jesus as a fraud and deceiver, conceived by Mary from an encounter with a Roman soldier. A parallel to this battle of words can be seen in the Dead Sea Scrolls. Here, the writings of the Jewish Qumran community contain many negative and vitriolic statements about their fellow Jews based in Jerusalem. All these writings need to be seen as products of their time, reflecting an internal struggle between groups vying for acceptance and credibility. Here too, we can see how the idea that Christianity superseded Judaism could take hold in such a powerful way.

When this dimension of Church history is neglected through the passage of time, the statements about Jews in the New Testament and the writings of the early Church are understood in isolation from their original context and become dangerous ammunition for later generations. This ammunition was fired during centuries of hatred, paving the way for the dreadful events of the Middle Ages, and eventually, for those of the twentieth century.

When the Nazis sought to justify their anti-Semitic campaign in the early decades of the twentieth century, they made use of the teaching and example of the Church. Despite the use of religious rhetoric to support the Nazi ideology, it would be wrong to regard Nazism as in any sense Christian (indeed, the Nazi plans included the eventual eradication of Christianity). It would also be wrong to confuse anti-Judaism (hostility to the Jewish religion) with anti-Semitism (hostility to Jews on the false but common assumption that they are a distinctive race). Even throughout the long and painful history of anti-Judaism, conversion to Christianity offered Jews a route out of social ostracism, however unappealing that route might be. Anti-Semitism offered no such option; practising Christians with Jewish ancestry were irretrievably tainted in the eyes of Nazism.

The Nazis were able to promote anti-Semitism by drawing both on a latent antipathy towards the Jews amongst German Christians, and on past practices and writings within the Church. Three instances stand out. It was the Fourth Lateran Council of 1215 that first required Jews to distinguish themselves from others by wearing distinctive clothing: in Germanic territory they were required to wear conical hats, and in Latin countries they wore a yellow badge (the colour symbolising the cowardice of Judas Iscariot, who betrayed Christ). The Nazis reintroduced this practice in Germany in 1939, requiring all Jews to wear yellow stars on their clothing. Secondly, it was the Synod of Breslau of 1267 that first specified that Jews could live only in segregated quarters in a city. Although Jewish neighbourhoods had long been common, this was the first time that segregation was enforced, and is therefore the first instance of a Jewish ghetto (although the term was coined following Jewish segregation in Venice in 1516). The Nazis also reintroduced Jewish ghettos in 1939.

Perhaps most disturbing of all was Hitler's appeal to Martin Luther in support of his argument for the 'final solution'. In 1523 Luther wrote: 'we [Christians] are but Gentiles, while the Jews are the image of Christ. We are aliens and in-laws; they are blood relatives, cousins and brothers of our Lord.'[9] But by 1542 Luther's attitude had changed. In his tract *Concerning the Jews and their Lies* he wrote: 'if they [the Jews] turn from their blasphemies we must gladly forgive them; but if not, we must not suffer them to remain.'[10] It was here that Hitler found theological support for his actions. Furthermore, Luther's 'advice' in his tract, 'that their synagogues should be burnt down', has a chilling parallel with the events of *Kristallnacht* on 9 and 10 November 1938, when organised anti-Jewish riots took place in Germany and Austria. *Kristallnacht* is regarded by many as the beginning of the Holocaust.

To appreciate the influence of anti-Judaism among German Christians one need look no further than to Dietrich Bonhoeffer. He is rightly remembered for his brave opposition to Nazism, the help that he gave to victims of the Nazi regime – including Jews – and his involvement in the failed plot to assassinate Hitler, which led to his arrest and execution. The courageous and scholarly Bonhoeffer, who is widely regarded as the great Christian martyr of the twentieth century, was considered for honour as a 'Righteous among the nations' at the Yad Vashem Holocaust Memorial in Jerusalem. And yet, as state anti-Semitism took hold in Germany, Bonhoeffer commented in a lecture in 1933:

> The [German] State's measures against Jewry are connected, how-ever, in a very special way with the Church. In the Church of Christ we have never lost sight of the idea that the 'chosen people', which placed the Saviour of the World on the Cross, must bear the curse of its actions through a long history of suffering.[11]

Such a statement sits uncomfortably alongside Bonhoeffer's later acts of compassion and bravery on behalf of Jews, and one can only specu-late as to how his thinking developed as the full horror of state anti-Semitism became clear. Bonhoeffer's example highlights how deeply embedded anti-Judaism had become within his own Christian tradition, and the tension this could cause in a person of faith and compassion.

In one important respect that long history of the suffering of the Jews has taken a turn for the better. The treatment of the Jews in Nazi Germany and the subsequent discovery of the horrors of the Holocaust caused the world – and not least the churches – to stop, think and take action. The relations between Christians and Jews have improved immeasurably since the dark decades of the early twentieth century.

In Britain, the Council of Christians and Jews was established in 1942 by the Archbishop of Canterbury and the Chief Rabbi to combat prejudice, intolerance, discrimination and anti-Semitism. Since then it has become an international movement. In 1965, the Roman Catholic Church made a decisive step in its document *Nostra Aetate* (*In Our Time*), expressing a distinctly positive attitude towards Judaism. This changed attitude is nowhere more apparent than in the Good Friday liturgy.[12] In the old Roman Catholic Missal the following collect appeared:

> Let us pray also for the unbelieving Jews:
> that our God and Lord will remove the veil from their hearts,
> so that they too may acknowledge our Lord Jesus Christ.

This was later replaced by:

> Let us pray for the Jewish people,
> the first to hear the word of God,
> that they may continue to grow in the love of his name
> and in faithfulness to his covenant.

Significantly, this change acknowledges that God's covenantal relationship with the Jewish people remains. In other words, it does not imply that this relationship was either broken as a result of the crucifixion, or superseded as a result of the emergence of the Christian Church. The prayer acknowledges instead a special relationship, a relationship that is also reflected now in the prayers of other Christian denominations. For instance, the Church of England's book *Lent, Holy Week and Easter* includes the following intercession in its Good Friday liturgy:

> Lord God of Abraham,
> bless the children of your covenant, both Jew and Christian;
> take from us all blindness and bitterness of heart,
> and hasten the coming of your kingdom,
> when Israel shall be saved,
> the Gentiles gathered in,
> and we shall dwell together in mutual love and peace
> under the one God and Father of our Lord Jesus Christ.

Other significant developments in Christian–Jewish relations have taken place in recent years that have gained considerable international attention. A new script was written for the 2000 production of the famous Oberammergau Passion Play. Previously the play had come in for much criticism for its anti-Jewish sentiment. Indeed, Hitler once said of the play:

> never has the menace of Jewry been so convincingly portrayed as in this presentation of what happened in the times of the Romans. There, one sees in Pontius Pilate a Roman racially and intellectually so superior that he stands out like a firm, clean rock in the middle of the whole muck and mire of Jewry.[13]

The new production emphasises the Jewishness of Jesus and his disciples, who wear skull-caps and prayer-shawls. The controversial blood curse uttered by the Jewish crowd has been removed, and the culpability of the Roman authorities in Jesus' execution is given greater emphasis than before.

Also in 2000, Pope John Paul II led the Roman Catholic Church in an act of repentance for its past wrongs, as described in the document *Memory and Reconciliation: the Church and the Faults of the Past*, which included the treatment of the Jews. This was no more powerfully symbolised than during the Pope's historic visit to Jerusalem that year, when he prayed for forgiveness at the Western Wall – the holiest site for Jews – placing a prayer written on a piece of paper into a crack in the wall. It was a simple act of profound significance towards those he called 'the people of the Covenant'.

So where does the painful history of Christian–Jewish relations and its improvement in recent years lead us in the early years of the twenty-first century?

Perhaps the first point to note is that there is still much that can be done to enhance Christian–Jewish relations by churches, not least from the lectern and pulpit or in Bible study groups. Each week passages are read from the New Testament that often include negative statements about 'the Jews' or 'the Pharisees' (a dominant Jewish group in the first century). It is easy to perpetuate this negative stereotype unless preachers and Bible study leaders address the issue of anti-Judaism and explain carefully the historical context in which the books of the New Testament were written. Similarly, as the changes in the Oberammergau Passion Play highlight, dramatic presentations of the Passion narrative, which might reinforce the mistaken idea that 'the

Jews' are responsible for Jesus' death, require careful thought and planning.

The painful history of Christian–Jewish relations as outlined in this chapter also needs to be taught if lessons from the past are to be learned and mistakes are not to be repeated. The potential for negative representations of 'the Jews' within Christianity to reinforce anti-Semitic sentiments remains a risk, and is something the churches should acknowledge and address. Holocaust Remembrance Day, introduced in Britain in 2001, provides an opportunity for churches in Britain to do just that.

A greater understanding of Christian–Jewish relations also helps to put in context the troubled recent history of the Middle East. It is all too easy to equate the state of Israel with Judaism, and for criticism of Israel's policies towards Palestinians to spill over into anti-Judaism or anti-Semitism. Just as 'the Jews' were wrongly and collectively blamed for Christ's death, so 'the Jews' cannot be held collectively responsible for the actions of a national government.

And there are wider lessons to be learnt from the history of Christian–Jewish relations. We live in an age where religious and cultural differences threaten world stability. Whether we like it or not, religion has re-emerged as a major force in politics. The history of Christian–Jewish relations provides a stark warning of what harm can be done in the name of religion. But more positively, the constructive dialogue that has taken place between Christians and Jews in recent decades provides both hope and a model for dialogue between other faith communities in the future. It provides hope in that, despite such a painful history, fruitful dialogue is possible. And it provides a model for how it can be achieved, and that is when the dialogue is not superficial, but is honest, open, and gets right to the heart of the matter.

It was the British writer William Norman Ewer who in the 1920s wrote this clerihew:

> How odd
> Of God
> To choose
> The Jews.

To which Cecil Browne famously replied:

> But not so odd
> As those who choose
> A Jewish God
> But spurn the Jews.

The spurning of Jews by Christians for many centuries is more than an oddity – it is both a scandal and a tragedy. It is also a warning – a warning of how a religion whose core ethic of love and forgiveness can harbour and justify prejudice and hatred.

It is only relatively recently, with the benefit of detailed studies of the society in which early Christianity emerged, that the anti-Jewish statements found in the New Testament and in the writings of the early Church Fathers have been seen in their proper historical context. When this is done, uncomfortable as these statements may be, they make sense. Taken out of context, they become divisive and dangerous.

Christ's first words from the cross also need to be placed in their historical context. But unlike those words of hostility and mistrust, they have a timeless quality, and they challenge us now. Perhaps the challenge they posed was too great for some who first heard it, and so they removed the words from Christ's lips. Or perhaps they recognised the significance of the challenge and so added them. Whatever the reason, the first of the seven last words speak powerfully about what has been done to the Jewish people in the name of Christ. Father, forgive us.

A MAN SITS ALONE AT A TABLE; he is writing. Stretched out before him are two scrolls. He is copying the words of one scroll onto the other, patiently and carefully. As he writes, he thinks and prays about the words he copies. This is no laborious chore, it is an act of loving devotion.

The words he has copied so far have confused, challenged, excited and inspired him. But now his mood has darkened: as the story before him unfolds it has taken him into the suffering of the one about whom he writes. This man has been crucified. Although the execution took place many years before, for the writer it could have been only yesterday, or even just a moment ago. And although all that he sees are words, in his mind's eye the writer believes he has just witnessed the terrible event.

The reason for such visceral, emotional intensity is that the person nailed to the cross dominates the writer's life: his prayers, his relationships, his judgements, his hopes and expectations. All that he does – all that he is – is in reference to that person about whom he writes.

What will he write next? Looking down, he sees that the completed scroll continues, 'And they cast lots to divide his clothing.' But another phrase has come to mind, a familiar phrase ascribed to that man on the cross and handed down by reliable witnesses: 'Father forgive them; for they know not what they do.'

He pauses. His sheer revulsion at the scene pictured in his mind pushes away thoughts of forgiveness – indeed, the image evokes feelings of powerlessness, frustration, hatred and revenge. And yet that phrase in his mind will not go away. It pulls him in another direction, challenging his instinctive feelings – just like so much he knows about that man. That compassionate, understanding, forgiving phrase seems so apt for the man about whom he writes – the man who gives meaning to his life.

He has a choice and must make a decision. What should he write next? He knows the importance of that phrase. He knows the effect that the presence or absence of those few words will have on those who read or hear what he writes. It is a difficult choice and an awesome responsibility. And so before he makes his decision he falls to his knees in prayer.

3

'Truly, I say to you, today you will be with me in Paradise' (Luke 23:43)

The Two Thieves (after Gillian Rose): Amon Goeth and Oskar Schindler

GILES FRASER

> The torture of a victim transforms the dangerous crowd into a public of ancient theater or of modern film, as captivated by the bloody spectacle as our contemporaries are by the horrors of Hollywood. When the spectators are satiated with the violence that Aristotle calls 'cathartic' – whether real or imaginary it matters little – they all return peaceably to their homes to sleep the sleep of the just.
>
> René Girard[1]

A bullfight, a war film, a boxing match or a public crucifixion: what are the ethics of 'watching'? Of course, we are never just watching. But what is the extent to which watching is participating? At what point do we become complicit? For surely not all watching is complicit: it is right that we watch the news, however terrible. There is no merit in turning away from the horror and violence that exists in the world. Likewise, there are films and novels that, through their depiction of violence, help us understand more fully its nature and reality. But when does the depiction of violence become a pornography of violence?

The term 'pornoviolence' was coined in the sixties in response to a spate of movies such as *Bonnie and Clyde* (1967) and *The Dirty Dozen* (1968) that combined extremes of violence with entertainment in an unprecedented way – or at least, in a way that was unprecedented in the film industry. For the combination of violence and entertainment is an ancient one that takes us back, not just to the Colosseum but also to the foot of the cross itself. Whatever else it was, crucifixion was a spectacle, designed to be seen. The suffering body is held up high, in a public place, carefully staged for maximum effect. Christ is crucified alongside two criminals. And people came from far and wide just to watch.

Film studies may seem an unlikely source of interesting theology, but it strikes me that it is precisely here that issues of voyeurism and complicity are given much intelligent attention. This is surely unsurprising, for in studying the dynamics of film one of the most important concerns is that of audience and audience reception. These questions are raised in other art forms, nonetheless it is at the movies that our position as voyeur is most acute. We sit in the dark. We can see but we are not ourselves seen. From this vantage point we have an access to those parts of life usually deemed especially private. From the dark we see people making love and people dying, and all in such minute detail or slow motion. Tom Wolfe in his essay 'Pornoviolence' reflects upon the American public's obsessive interest in the film of John F. Kennedy's assassination: 'There has been an incessant replay, with every recoverable clinical detail, of those less than five seconds in which a man got his head blown off.' Wolfe points out that the perspective of the audience is the 'view from Oswald's rifle'. He goes on: 'The camera angle, therefore the viewer, is with the gun, the fist and the rock . . . You do not live the action through the hero's eyes. You live with the aggressor, whoever he may be.'[2]

In this short essay I want to explore some of the cross-over issues between film studies and theology as they pertain to our perspective as onlookers before the cross. I have chosen to do this through an examination of a characteristically insightful and maddeningly difficult article by Gillian Rose on the various ways in which the Holocaust is represented in the movies. Rose's essay offers a point of departure with which to address the complex concerns of voyeurism and identification that make the whole business of watching a film about the Holocaust problematic. The questions are these: With whom do we identify in the film? How does the film-maker elicit our sympathies? And, more importantly, are they elicited in such a way as to make us feel comfortable or uncomfortable about the experience of watching the film? Am I convicted or sheltered by the film's depiction of the horror of the Holocaust? My suggestion will be that the sensitivities these questions give rise to have a very real potency when transferred to the foot of the cross. Furthermore, by exploring the dynamics of voyeurism and identification in the very different context of the Holocaust we are, hopefully, more able to think about issues of theological concern without reaching for the standard answers which can mask the moral complexity of Good Friday.

Rose asks us first to consider the way in which the Holocaust is represented in the film *Schindler's List* (1993). Directed by Stephen Spielberg after a book by Thomas Keneally, *Schindler's List* tells the story of how German war profiteer Oskar Schindler came to save more than a thousand Jews from the death-camps, risking his life and losing his fortune in the process. The film won seven academy awards and received huge popular acclaim. It has been widely used in schools as a teaching aid and consequently, for a whole generation, *Schindler's List* has become one of the most influential points of access for understanding the horrors of the Holocaust.

A number of critics, however, have faulted the film's oversimplification of complex moral issues. Bryan Cheyette, in a review for the *Times Literary Supplement*, calls *Schindler's List* 'a seductive and self-confident narrative' that has 'no real understanding of the difficulties inherent in representing the ineffable'. The book from which the film derives is likewise attacked for 'glibly assimilat[ing] . . . an unimaginable past in a breathtakingly untroubled manner'. Cheyette goes on to compare *Schindler's List* unfavourably to Claude Lanzmann's seven-and-a-half-hour documentary *Shoah* which is said to be 'intellectually scrupulous and does not try to represent history in a facile series of cinematic tropes'.[3] At one point in *Shoah*, Lanzmann interviews a barber working in his shop in Tel Aviv. The barber is pressed by Lanzmann to tell the story of how he shaved the heads of friends and neighbours immediately before they were forced into the showers and gassed. The barber starts the story but, as he recalls his friends, he finds it impossible to go on. Obviously in great distress, the barber asks for the camera to be turned off. He can't continue. Instead, however, Lanzmann lets the camera roll on. The barber cannot speak, but the film continues to be shot. Lanzmann's cruelty contrasts markedly with Spielberg's sympathy – and yet, the barber's inability to speak indicates levels of pain that the smoothly flowing narrative of Spielberg's film is wholly unable to capture.

Cheyette is not alone in wanting to claim that the Holocaust is so utterly terrible that nothing is able to capture its horror, that we are forced into silence by its very magnitude. Adorno famously asserted there could be no more poetry after Auschwitz. For many theologians, the very prospect of a *logos* of mass death seems entirely inappropriate – what is needed is silent prayer, not speculative theology. We need to cry, not speak. The Holocaust, like the cross itself, leads many of us into silence.

But there are very real problems with the silence too. Imagine the following: I am out doing my shopping and I see a neighbour coming towards me. I know that she has just lost a child in a tragic cot death. Panic sets in. What do I say? What is there to say? Better to say nothing than come out with embarrassed clichés. Better to opt for silence. I slip down the next aisle and pass by unnoticed. Silence seems somehow altogether more profound than nervous chatter. And yet, of course, it is my blushes that are being spared here. It is my fear at confronting the pain of cot death that leads me to silence. For, as Rose sets out to expose, silence can also be yet one more form of avoidance, a subtle and persuasive strategy to help us overlook the horror.

> To argue for silence, prayer, the banishment equally of poetry and knowledge, in short the witness of 'ineffability', that is, non-representability, is to mystify something we dare not understand, because we fear that it may be all too understandable, all too continuous with what we are – human, all too human.[4]

We often sit in silence before the cross. And for many of us silence is the only appropriate response to its horror. We have nothing to say. Silence is respectful. Not only that, but it somehow seems that only silence has the sort of *gravitas* that can match the seriousness of the subject. Rose challenges us that this silence may, on occasions, reflect a false piety purchased far too cheaply. Too often something has not been faced. But what? In the liturgy of Holy Week we begin by welcoming Christ into the city. Often the congregation are cast as the crowd: 'Hosanna in the highest' we cry out. It is this self-same crowd who will be jeering and spitting before the week is out: 'Crucify him.' What is hard for us to face is the suspicion that we too would have betrayed Christ in similar circumstances. We can sit before the cross and think how terrible it is that they have murdered our Lord. Or one can count oneself amongst the murderers, swept up in the frenzy of the mob, too afraid to speak out, ready to go along with what the authorities decide.

In a famous scene from the film, Schindler witnesses the liquidation of the ghetto. He sits astride his horse on a hill overlooking the ghetto and is horrified by the brutality and violence unfolding before him. Prompted by his girlfriend, he has to look away. And that's my/our reaction too: I feel ill and want to hide behind the sofa. Like Schindler, the viewer watches the film from some safe distance. And that, precisely, is the problem with the film. In *Schindler's List* the place from which I watch the film is never fully challenged. I am not asked to examine my own potential for viciousness, I am never provoked to think whether I too would have become a camp bully or a silent coward. The perspective from the sofa, like that from the hill-top promontory, is sheltered from the threat of moral or spiritual interrogation. From the sofa 'our complacency is left in place and willfully reinforced'.

In *Schindler's List* we are presented with two archetypes, Oskar Schindler and Amon Goeth, the two thieves of my sub-title. Like the two thieves crucified alongside Christ, these two represent, as it were, the good criminal and the bad criminal. Schindler, the war profiteer who gives all his money away to save his Jewish workforce, and Goeth, the suave psychopath for whom murder is entertainment. In many ways Schindler and Goeth are portrayed as being very similar: both enjoy money, women, parties, good food, 'Both Austrian Catholics from undistinguished families, they are said to be each other's "dark brother".' Rose goes on to comment:

> The comparison makes the reader's task harder in figuring out the reasons for the difference between what Keneally cynically calls their 'reversible appetites', the difference in the individual outcome of their common origins. Such plasticity of history, such pragmatics of good and evil, such continuity between the banality of Schindler's benevolence and the gratuity of Goeth's violence should mean the reader, and *pari passu*, the audience, experience the crisis of identity in their own breasts. Instead we enjoy vicarious revulsion at the handsome sadist, Goeth . . . and we applaud the *bon vivant* Schindler in his precarious outwitting of him.[5]

For all its dramatic realism about the horrors of human suffering, *Schindler's List* is a feel-good film. Though we may cry and be appalled by the brutality of Nazi genocide, after the film we can all return to our beds and sleep the sleep of the just. Rose, however, thinks we ought to be provoked into a 'crisis of identity in our own breasts'.

Part of what is at stake here is our frequent refusal to face our own potential for wickedness.

> We try to avoid 'owning' our bad motives, not just from vanity (though this is important) but because we feel that to own or acknowledge is to accept. We dread exposure to the hidden force whose power we sense. Our official idea of ourselves has no room for it . . .

writes Mary Midgely in her excellent book *Wickedness: A Philosophical Essay*.[6] Self-deception arises 'because we see motives which are in fact our own as alien to us and refuse to acknowledge them'.[7] Instead we invent stories where the wickedness is embodied by another: an alien, a monstrous other, a foreigner, a Nazi with a funny accent. In refusing to acknowledge our 'shadow' − to use Jungian vocabulary − we give it more power, the power of working unchecked in the dark. Rose's point is that sometimes that darkness is called silence − the place beyond interrogation.

The great story of the dangers of self-avoidance is, as Midgely points out, Stevenson's *The Strange Case of Dr Jekyll and Mr Hyde*. The story is, in part, about the dangers of pious self-righteousness. Dr Jekyll so refuses to acknowledge his darker side that it takes on a life of its own beyond the confines of his own self-image. Jekyll's concern for his own good character gives him no room to acknowledge his own Hyde-like tendencies. Consequently, they go unchecked: Mr Hyde is a consequence of Dr Jekyll's vanity. Similarly, we are commonly so unwilling to face our own potential for wickedness that, instead of squaring up to it and challenging it, we simply try to forget it or pretend it isn't there. This means that the dangerous part of ourselves is able to work unchecked. The appropriate and necessary 'crisis of identity' comes when one discovers that Jekyll and Hyde are different sides to the same person – and not two different people.

Christian people are, I think, often particularly susceptible to this sort of splitting. We are supposed to be good, kind and gentle, etc. Our official self-image has no room for an acknowledgement of our own greedy, petty, revengeful secrets. There is a certain sort of 'Christian smile' that makes me shudder. For this smile is frequently a tell-tale sign of the presence of Mr Hyde – or, what Nietzsche called *ressentiment*. My two thieves, Goeth and Schindler, are not two but one: this is the message that ought to strike us as a 'crisis of identity'.

One of the most challenging recent accounts of the Holocaust is that of Christopher Browning in his *Ordinary Men: Reserve Police Battalion 101 and the Final Solution in Poland*. These 'ordinary men' were not career Nazis or Goeth-type psychopaths; they were policemen, too old to be of much use to the army and consequently not subject to the same intensity of ideological indoctrination as, for instance, members of the *Einsatzgruppen* units. These were not men chosen as particularly suitable for the task of cold-blooded murder. They were, as it were, you and I. And yet, in the July of 1942, Reserve Police Battalion 101 came to the Polish village of Józefów and shot some 1500 Jews, mostly women, children and the elderly.

> Departing from Bilgoraj around 2:00 a.m., the truck convoy arrived in Józefów just as the sky was beginning to lighten. [Major] Trapp assembled his men in a half-circle and addressed them. After explaining the battalion's murderous assignment, he

made his extraordinary offer: any of the older men who did not feel up to the task that lay before them could step out. Trapp paused, and after some moments one man from Third Company, Otto-Julius Schimke stepped forward. Captain Hoffmann . . . was furious that one of his men had been the first to break ranks. Hoffmann began to berate Schimke, but Trapp cut him off. After he had taken Schimke under his protection, some ten or twelve other men stepped forward as well. They turned in their weapons and were told to await further instructions.[8]

What is so extraordinary about this account is the permission Trapp gives for his soldiers to absent themselves from the task ahead. Further, what is even more extraordinary is that only 'some ten or twelve' came forward out of a group of roughly 500 'ordinary men'. More men dropped out as the day's murder progressed. August Zorn recalls the circumstances of his decision not to continue:

I only reached the execution site when my comrades had already shot their Jews. At the sight of his countrymen who had been shot, my Jew threw himself on the ground and remained lying there. I then cocked my carbine and shot him in the back of the head. Because I was already very upset from the cruel treatment of the Jews during the clearing of the town and was completely in turmoil, I shot too high. The entire back of the skull of my Jew was torn off and the brain exposed. Parts of the skull flew into Sergeant Steinmetz's face. This was grounds for me, after returning to the truck, to go to the first sergeant and ask for my release. I had become so sick that I simply couldn't continue anymore. I was then replaced by the first sergeant.[9]

Quite a number, like Zorn, excused themselves from duties after having experienced the full reality of what they had been asked to do. Even so, only about 10 per cent of the Battalion declined to go on. And this, of course, raises the question about the other 90 per cent. Often we imagine that many went along with orders out of fear for their own safety or that of their families. But this does not seem to have been a factor here. Given that these were not fanatical ideological anti-Semites, and given the lack of coercion, why did so many of these 'ordinary

men' participate in the murders at Józefów? The book ends with
the chilling question: 'If the men of Reserve Police Battalion 101
could become killers under such circumstances, what group of men
cannot?'[10]

With whom do we identify in the story of the crucifixion? Where do
we place ourselves in the action? What would we 'ordinary' men and
women be up to on that day? 'If the men of Reserve Police Battalion
101 could become killers under such circumstances, what group of
men cannot?'

The sort of film Rose wants about the Holocaust would work so as to
reveal our own complicity in the patterns of life and thought that make
the Holocaust possible. A film that encourages us to empathise with a
member of the SS, where we are led to 'identify with his hopes and
fears, disappointments and rage, so that when it comes to killing, we
put our hands on the trigger with him, wanting him to get what he
wants.' Of course, the problem with this sort of film is that we now
know, in advance, how the story of the SS man will go and so our
identification with such a character would be easy to resist. The same,
of course, is true of the sort of film I would like to make about the
crucifixion. In it we are led to identify with Pilate. We are encouraged
to see things from his point of view, we are shown the forces that moti-
vate him. And when it comes to the moment of condemnation, we also
wash our hands and turn our backs.

In fact, W. H. Auden has done something very similar (though with
a comic twist) in his For the Time Being. Here Herod is lamenting the birth
of Christ and reflecting on what a disaster will follow the arrival of this
baby. In the monologue Herod explains how much he has done for
this backward and superstitious province. Things, he reflects, have been
getting better:

> Barges are unloading soil fertilizer at the river wharves. Soft drinks
> and sandwiches may be had in the inns at reasonable prices.
> Allotment gardening has become popular. The highway to the
> coast goes straight up over the mountains and the truck-drivers no
> longer carry guns. Things are beginning to take shape. It's a long
> time since anyone stole a park bench or murdered the swans. There

are children in this province who have never seen a louse, shop-keepers who have never handled a counterfeit coin, women of forty who have never hidden in a ditch except for fun. Yes, in twenty years I have managed to do a little. Not enough, of course. There are still villages only a few miles from here where they still believe in witches. There isn't a single town where a good book-shop would pay . . . Still it's a beginning. In the twenty years the darkness has been pushed back a little.[11]

What Herod fears is the barbaric imagination in which 'Mongolian idiots are regarded as sacred and mothers who give birth to twins are instantly put to death, where malaria is treated by yelling . . . where the best cuts of meat are reserved for the dead.'[12] He wants an ordered, sane and reasonable society. And then these three weird mystics turn up with talk of the birth of God. Herod imagines the disastrous chaos that will ensue. He doesn't like violence but he is in an impossible position, being responsible for the welfare of so many. With great reluctance he orders the massacre of the innocents. He concludes: 'I'm a liberal. I want everybody to be happy. I wish I had never been born.'[13] It's not too hard to see how a similar narrative could be constructed around Pilate.

For Rose, the film that helps us see the potential for fascist ideology within ourselves – or at least, our potential for complicity with those forces that bring it about – is the Merchant-Ivory production of Kazuo Ishiguro's *Remains of the Day*. Set in an upper-class English household in the 1920s, the film explores the complicity of Stevens, the head butler, a man dedicated to service, with the Nazi-supporting lord whose employ he is in. For Stevens, his master's decision to sack his Jewish chambermaids leads to a 'crisis of identity'. Stevens' life was his work, that of service to his lord and master. His whole identity is bound up with the organisation of his master's household and is premised upon a sense of the good judgement of his lord.

> The attractions of German Nazism are present in microcosm in the organisation of the aristocratic household as a fascist corporation. The members of the corporation are free in their initial pledge of loyalty, but become unfree in their consequent total rescinding of the right to criticise.[14]

Rose does not, as it happens, draw out the theological possibilities of her reading of *Remains of the Day*, but they are clear enough to see. For just as the pledge of loyalty to a whole pattern of life defined by the 1920s aristocratic English household can render one incapable of critical and self-critical reflection, so too the pledge of loyalty to a heavenly Lord, a Lord even further beyond scrutiny, can lead to an incapacity to reflect upon the ethics of the Christian life. If we are in God's service, then all that issues from that service must be morally justified. Critical and (what Rowan Williams has elsewhere called) 'self-critical vigilance' is thus switched off. As the previous chapter has shown, the consequences of any lack of critical vigilance can be dreadful. The expulsion of the Jewish chambermaids from Lord Darlington's household is a parallel to the expulsion of Jews from Christian society – the final solution of which is the Holocaust. I have in my study a photograph of a German bishop, clearly having just come out of church and in full clerical garb, giving the Nazi salute. I keep it there to remind me of the need for self-critical vigilance.

Gillian Rose was received into the Church of England on her deathbed by the then Bishop of Coventry. Her last words, written in a bedside notebook, were: 'Keep your mind in hell and d N' – keep your mind in hell and despair not. That, I take it, is the condition of prayerfulness before the foot of the cross. We must not seek the easy escape from hell, though many are on offer. We must not be voyeurs of Christ's suffering, watching from the dark and safe place that is beyond the difficult and painful lens of self-critical vigilance.

> The ultimate predator is not suspended in a saddle on a charger, overlooking from a promontory, with a piquant revulsion, with the ancient, exultant sense of abomination, such as, in a mediaeval painting the just show for the damned, or joining the queue of survivors. Instead of emerging with sentimental tears, which leave us emotionally and politically intact, we emerge with the dry eyes of deep grief, which belongs to the recognition of our ineluctable grounding in the norms of the emotional and political culture represented, and which leaves us with the uncertainty of the remains of the day.[15]

Is that how the disciples felt as they watched Jesus die? Broken, confused, compromised, ashamed – but with the remains of the day, the beginnings of the kingdom.

THIS IS NOT A MEDITATION for now. This is a meditation for next time you watch a film that deals with violence or has a lot of violence in it — significantly, that gives you a very wide choice. Here are some of the questions to have in mind:

Does the film make violence seem innocuous? Famously, nobody ever died in *The A-team*. There were many explosions, constant use of automatic weapons, frequent car crashes etc., but nobody ever died. Presumably, this was intended to make the use of guns and grenades more acceptable to a younger audience. But what is the effect on such an audience? Does it carry the message that violence isn't real? Reflect upon whether, and in what ways, the film you are watching tries to cover up violence or render it innocuous. Or perhaps there is a coyness or sentimentality about violence, thus rendering it partially invisible. Why?

Of course, many films do not cover up violence at all. Some films aim to be 'realistic' in the portrayal of blood and guts. I think of *Reservoir Dogs* or *Black Hawk Down*. But is this 'realism' a way of celebrating an aesthetic of death or mutilation? Is the film titillated by the dreadful things we can do to each other or by showing how terribly we can die?

Be conscious of the ways in which our sympathies as the viewer are elicited. How does the film-maker encourage us to identify with various characters, thus, perhaps desensitising our critical judgement? Would we see James Bond as a cruel psychopath if it weren't for his good looks, witty asides, or a sense that he is 'on the right side'? Is violence made legitimate because the target is an alien? Try to disrupt the spell cast by all the narrative and cinematic tricks up the director's sleeve. Spin different imaginative tales. For instance, if there is a casual death depicted in the film, imagine a family for that person, imagine them as a child, etc. Don't let yourself be railroaded by the plot or by the encouragement to identify with the heroes or heroines rather than the villains.

Also, have a sense of how the film appeals in its depiction of violence. Be aware of being entertained. Be aware of being fascinated. Be aware of being amused. Above all be honest with yourself.

So as to contextualise this particular way of watching, how about starting the film and ending it by saying to yourself:

If we say we have no sin we deceive ourselves
and the truth is not in us,
if we confess our sins God is faithful and just,
and will forgive us our sins
and cleanse us from all unrighteousness.

Almighty God, our heavenly Father,
we have sinned against you and against our neighbour
in thought and word and deed,
through negligence, through weakness,
through our own deliberate fault.
We are truly sorry and repent of all our sins.
For the sake of your Son Jesus Christ, who died for us,
forgive us all that is past
and grant that we may serve you in newness of life
to the glory of your name. Amen.

4

'Woman, behold your son! . . . Behold, your mother!' (John 19:26f)

PETER DOLL

A fashionably dressed young woman recently walked into a high-street jewellery shop and went to the counter. 'I'd like to buy a cross to put on this necklace.' The shop assistant placed a tray of small crosses on the counter. The customer looked at them and then asked, 'Do you have one without the little man?'

While most people today can still recognise the cross as the primary Christian symbol, there are many like that young woman who know little, if anything, about its Christian meaning and for whom it is primarily a fashion statement. Even for committed Christians, the ubiquity of the cross may mean that it has lost its power to move or shock.

For the medieval Christian, however, the cross was a presence that accompanied every step of the journey of life from the moment an infant was baptised and signed with the cross. The cross was there in church, in the home, in the market-place, and even the roads were marked by a succession of wayside crosses. Signing oneself with the cross was universally used as a mark of devotion, and when people swore, they did so by the cross and by the wounds that it inflicted on Jesus.

But in communities throughout medieval England there was one particular image of the cross that served as a primary focus, and that was the great rood (from the Old English for 'cross', *rod*) that stood in the chancel arch of every church. Even in churches that were crowded with images of all kinds, the rood presided over and defined the symbolism. In the midst of each church was a stone or wooden screen between the nave (the people's part of the building) and the chancel (the clergy's part, where the high altar stood and where Christ was present in the reserved Sacrament hanging above the altar). Typically the bottom of the screen was solid, panelled with painted images of the saints. The middle section was open, giving a clear view into the chancel to the altar. On top of the screen was a loft supporting the great rood, which bore the image of the crucified Christ, with the Blessed Virgin Mary and St John the Evangelist (who is often identified as the 'beloved disciple' mentioned in John's Gospel) standing at the foot of the cross on either side. The figures formed a tableau of this third of Christ's last words. When every church was understood as a microcosm of all creation, as a place where heaven and earth came together, the rood screen marked the juncture, the threshold between the earthly realm of the nave and the heavenly realm of the chancel.

The cross was not simply the focus of everyday life and of the sacred geography of the church building. For Christians it came to symbolise the focal event of the history of the world. Each parish community enacted this belief in its veneration of the cross in the ceremonies of Holy Week, in particular the Palm Sunday procession. After a procession of the Blessed Sacrament around the outside of the church – commemorating Jesus' triumphal entry into Jerusalem – clergy and people came to the west door of the church. The whole community then entered and gathered before the rood screen. All through Lent an enormous veil, painted with the symbols of Christ's passion, hung suspended before the great rood. The crucifix was now triumphantly revealed; the whole parish knelt down before it, and the anthem '*Ave, Rex Noster*', 'Hail, our King', was sung as the clergy venerated the cross by kissing the ground beneath it:

Hail, our King, Son of David, Thou the World's Redeemer, whom the prophets testified should come unto the house of Israel, to be their Saviour. For Thou in truth wast sent from the Father unto us to be our saviour, for whom the righteous in all ages from the beginning have been waiting. And now Hosanna to the Son of David: Blessed is he that cometh in the name of the Lord: Hosanna in the highest.[1]

The people in every parish in the land celebrated the crucifixion of Christ as the centre of the history of the world – the crux, the turning-point. The downward trajectory of humanity since the Fall in the Garden of Eden was decisively reversed. From the cross onwards, God's people were irrevocably drawn upwards towards his heavenly kingdom.

The great rood was a representation of the very moment of Christ's utterance of the third of his last words from the cross. John's Gospel records, 'When Jesus saw his mother, and the disciple whom he loved standing near, he said to his mother, "Woman, behold, your son!" Then he said to the disciple, "Behold, your mother!" And from that hour the disciple took her to his own home' (19:26–27). For those who follow Christ in the way of faith, this encounter between Jesus, Mary and John in the crucifixion is an important moment of decision and transition. It is a time when Christ looks beyond the torments he is suffering in the present to the future of those who have remained faithful to him and who are to be his future presence in the world. He prepares them for the inauguration of the new community of the Church, in which the old ways of relationship based on family ties and ethnicity give way to a different mode of being. Those faithful to Jesus, from whatever background, will relate to one another as brothers and sisters, parents and children, united by Christ's saving passion and death into his resurrection life.

From whatever perspective we look at the cross, whether that of the whole of human history or that of our own individual journeys through life, the cross stands at a crossroad for each of us. We may choose between keeping to the same path – our old way of life – or we can opt for a new direction. The first way embraces this mortal life and will end in death. The other way demands our dying to this world in order to win a new and everlasting life.

Each time we encounter Christ on the cross we come to this cross-road, to this time of decision. In truth, we spend a great deal of our life here. Our daily routine involves a series of such encounters. We live constantly on a threshold, as we have to make choices which define our citizenship in the city of humanity and in the City of God. A popular medieval treatise on the Ten Commandments, *Dives et Pauper*, explained the rationale for roadside crosses in this way: 'For this reason ben Crosses by ye waye, that whan folke passynge see the Crosse, they sholde thynke on Hym that deyed on the Crosse, and worshypp Hym above all thynge.'[2] When we see the cross, we are confronted with a choice: will we choose to take up our own cross and follow Christ towards his kingdom, or will we choose to pass by on the other side, to look after our interests in this world? The decision we are called to make finds its origins deep in the human psyche and as far back in human history as we can go. According to the Bible, it goes back to another tree and to our very first ancestors – to Adam and Eve's encounter with the tree of the knowledge of good and evil in the Garden of Eden (Gen. 2:15–3:24).

According to this account of creation, God made humanity in his own image and likeness, to be his representatives and to be like him. God gave Adam and Eve freedom of choice in all things and imposed on them only one restriction: they should not eat of the fruit of the tree of the knowledge of good and evil, for if they did they would lose their immortality and be subject to death. As the tree of the cross does now, so this first tree offered humanity a choice. Even within this one stric-ture imposed upon them, Adam and Eve remained free to choose to disobey God. When Satan as a serpent tempted them, telling them that if they ate they would be (even more) like God, Adam and Eve found their desire for power more compelling than God's commandment, and they ate. They came to the tree and they made the choice that, accord-ing to Christian tradition, lost for humanity our immortality and the life of paradise. And even if Adam and Eve never existed historically, the choice they made haunts the psyche of humanity. For we human beings have, now as then, a choice between life and death: of choosing to live at peace with our neighbours, of providing for the helpless and the needy, of tending and nurturing this creation which has been given to us to sustain our life. Yet throughout history we have chosen to make war, to be selfish, to exploit one another and the creation. Are we then as a species incapable of choosing life over death?

Despite humanity's failure to learn from the tragedies and disasters of history, we nevertheless remain dimly aware that God intends us for something else and holds out to us another way. Even among the secularly minded, this hope manifests itself in a belief in the perfectibility of humanity through technological and material progress. But those of the community of faith continue to be haunted by the 'memory' of that first tree and of the choice made by Adam and Eve. We are wounded in our inmost being, and we give no evidence of being able to heal ourselves. Only God, we believe, can heal us, and the story of our Scriptures is that of a God who seeks to restore human beings to the fullness of their humanity and to perfect his image within them.

In order to be healed, however, we need to deal with the legacy of the first tree and the wound it has imprinted on humanity. Within the plan of God, it would take the fruit of another tree to heal the wound of the first. This process is subtly attuned to human psychology, for when we human beings are frightened or wounded, in order to find healing and peace it is necessary for us to confront our fears. When a child falls off a bicycle, only by getting up and trying again can she overcome the fear instilled by the first fall. Likewise, for an adult who fails or suffers disappointment, there is the temptation to give in and count oneself a failure; but there is healing in the very process of making a new start and trying again. When we confront the cross, we are confronting our most fundamental fear – the fear of death. And yet God intends that through this encounter we should recover the greatest gift of all – that of eternal life in him.

The writers of the Hebrew Scriptures perceived early on such a pattern of healing through confrontation. In Genesis, the serpent is portrayed as being instrumental in the Fall of humanity from Eden. In the Book of Numbers, when the Israelites were in the wilderness, the Lord sent fiery serpents to punish their disobedience. When the people repented their sin, the Lord ordered Moses to make a serpent of bronze and to set it up on a pole, and those who looked on it were cured (21:6–9). In this way another instrument of death, and a reminder of the Fall of humanity, became a means of life. As the Wisdom of Solomon later reflected on this saving act:

> For the one who turned towards it was saved, not by the thing that
> was beheld, but by you, the Saviour of all . . . For neither herb nor
> poultice cured them, but it was your word, O Lord, that heals all
> people. For you have power over life and death; you lead mortals
> down to the gates of Hades and back again (16:7, 12–13).

In John's Gospel, the brazen serpent in turn became a prophetic sign
of the saving work on the cross of Christ himself, the one who broke
down the gates of Hades to release the souls imprisoned there: 'And
as Moses lifted up the serpent in the wilderness, so must the Son of
Man be lifted up, that whoever believes in him may have eternal life'
(3:14).

Jesus faced the same choice that confronts every human being on the
journey of life. Adam, the first archetypal man, chose disobedience to
God at the first tree and lost for humankind the life of paradise. Christ,
the second Adam, came to his own tree and faced the temptation of
shirking his vocation (Matt. 26:39). But because he chose the path of
obedience to God's will, he healed the sin of Adam, showing all
humanity the way back to Eden, back to the unity of the Father's love.

The earliest Christian documents recognised that God in Christ was
undoing the sin of Adam and restoring humanity to the eternal life of
paradise. St Paul wrote in his first letter to the Corinthians, 'For since
death came through a human being, the resurrection of the dead has
also come through a human being; for as all die in Adam, so all will be
made alive in Christ' (15:21–22). Within God's plan for the restoration
of creation and the salvation of every human being, the cross stands on
the boundary between earth and heaven, and it is only by the cross that
we might pass from one to the other.

Theologians of the early Church perceived in greater detail the pattern at work. As the outstanding preacher and paschal theologian St
John Chrysostom asserted, 'Christ conquered the devil using the very
means by which the devil conquered us: Christ took up the weapons
with which the devil had fought, and defeated him.'[3] Because the one
who was sinless accepted the penalty of humanity's sin, he transformed
the instrument of torture and death into an instrument of victory over
sin and death and of salvation for all God's people. Christ halted
humanity's fall into sin and death by raising us up with him on the

cross of his victory. Chrysostom gives a marvellous account of the divine healing at work on the cross:

> Can you now see how the very circumstances in which the devil conquered us have become the pattern of his own defeat? At the foot of the tree the devil overcame Adam; at the foot of the tree Christ vanquished the devil. As a result of the first tree humankind were consigned to Hades; now a second Adam calls back to life even those who had already descended there. The first tree hid a man who knew himself to have been undermined and stripped bare; the second tree displays the naked victor for all the world to see. The first death condemned those who were born after it; but this second death gives life even to those who were born before it. Who can describe sufficiently the mighty deeds of the Lord? For by his death we have become immortal. Such are the glorious deeds of the cross.[4]

As the cult of the cross developed in the Middle Ages, the scriptural typology that linked the tree of the Fall and the tree of salvation bore rich and exotic growths. For the sake of popular consumption, it was no longer enough that the two should be joined spiritually and symbolically. Pious imagery, local folklore, and the medieval love of miracles bound the two together physically as well, so that the wood of the cross descended directly from the tree in Eden. The *Golden Legend*, a history of the saints compiled by Jacobus de Voragine in the 1260s, tells how the seeds from the tree of the knowledge of good and evil were placed in the mouth of Adam when he died. The tree that grew up over Adam's grave was later cut down by King Solomon and used to bridge a pond. When the Queen of Sheba passed by that way, she saw in a vision that the Saviour of the World was to hang on that wood. Solomon then had the wood taken out and buried 'in the deepest bowels of the earth'. But a healing pond later welled up on that spot, and when the time of Christ's suffering drew near, the wood floated to the surface of the pond and was used to make Christ's cross. The Empress Helena, mother of the Emperor Constantine, whose vision of the cross gave him victory at the battle of the Milvian Bridge, later found the wood. It was identified as the wood of the True Cross when its power brought a dead youth back to life. Thus the wood of the cross was seen to bind together the wonders of creation and the incarnation; because God himself became a part of his creation in Christ, so the power of his resurrection might be conveyed by ordinary matter, by the water of baptism, by the bread and wine of the Eucharist, by the wood of the cross. No matter what was done to that wood, its power could no more be suppressed than could the resurrection life of Christ.

The choice offered us by God through the cross is just as irrepressible as that wood of the cross. No matter what we do with our lives, Christ comes to us, bidding us to take up our cross. Our choice is no less than that of death through clinging to this life or of eternal life through clinging to the death of Christ on the cross. As St Paul writes in the letter to the Philippians, 'I want to know Christ and the power of his resurrection and the sharing of his sufferings by becoming like him in his death' (3:10). The cross that is the crossroad of the history of the world is also a personal crossroad, a choice between life and death, for every individual who encounters Christ there.

If the decision to embrace the cross of Christ is the end of one journey, it is just the beginning of another, greater, pilgrimage, which marks an entirely new way of being human. Embracing the cross of Christ does not bring choices to an end. Rather, life becomes a pilgrimage in which we continue to encounter wayside crosses along the road. Each cross reminds us of our existence on that threshold of choice; each cross challenges us to follow Christ's or some other path. In this life we cannot move decisively and finally over from one side of the rood screen to the other. The Christian life is a journey made with Mary and John at the foot of the rood, a journey on the threshold, with one foot always on earth and the other always in heaven. Only in the fullness of God's time will we stand with both feet on the other side of the rood, soul and body in union with God.

The original sense of being a pilgrim was of having this status of a 'resident alien'. The understanding that Christians are 'strangers and foreigners on the earth' (Heb. 11:13) whose true citizenship is in heaven is firmly rooted in the New Testament (Phil. 3:20; Eph. 2:19; Heb. 13:14). According to this ideal, pilgrimage could be seen not as a journey to a particular geographical place, but as a voluntary exile from one's native land. In just this way did Abraham forsake his own country and kindred in obedience to the Lord's command (Gen. 12:1).

Even Moses, who spoke to God face to face as to a friend, was destined to wander in the wilderness and never quite attain the Promised Land (Num. 20:12). Christ himself undertook such a pilgrim journey during the forty days he spent in the wilderness following his baptism by John (Mark 1:13; Matt. 4; Luke 4). On the threshold of embracing his vocation as the Messiah, Christ was tempted by Satan to put aside that calling or to take a short-cut to his destiny. Jesus in his own earthly pilgrimage was tempted in every way as we are, yet without sin (Heb. 4:15).

In emulation of these examples, Irish monks in the sixth and following centuries, such as St Columba and St Columbanus, embarked on perpetual pilgrimages for the love of God and for the sake of proclaiming the Gospel to distant peoples. This tradition of pilgrimage continued in the Eastern Church into the nineteenth century, immortalised in the anonymous book *The Way of a Pilgrim*, which describes the experiences of a Russian peasant who tramped from place to place reciting the Jesus Prayer ('Lord Jesus Christ, Son of God, have mercy on me').

Alongside the tradition of the wandering pilgrimage, from very early in the history of the Church the practice of pilgrimage to particular places developed as well. This could be a journey to the shrine of a local saint, like that of St Frideswide in Oxford or St Wite in Devon, or to places of national significance, such as the shrine of St Thomas Becket in Canterbury or that of Our Lady of Walsingham. The commitment of Christians to walking in the way of the cross of their incarnate Lord also led many of them to Jerusalem and the Holy Land, to seek out the very places associated with Christ's earthly life and ministry, from the site of the stable in Bethlehem to the life-giving tomb in Jerusalem. For those unable to make the journey to Palestine and who wanted to walk the way of the cross at home, the devotion of the Stations of the Cross developed in the Middle Ages under Franciscan influence. The journey of faith to God's kingdom in this way became inseparably associated with pilgrimage to the cross.

Whether the pilgrimage is a simple wandering or a journey to a particular place, all pilgrimages share common features associated with our response to the cross and the consequent greater journey to God's kingdom. These features include *separation*, *existence on the threshold*, and the *holy place* that is the goal of the pilgrimage, and with them the pilgrimage would encapsulate within a particular journey the qualities of that greater journey that is the whole of a Christian life.

When Jesus explained to his disciples what following him entailed, he said, 'If any want to become my followers, let them deny themselves and take up their cross and follow me' (Matt. 16:24). Within the greater journey of Christian life, separation comes to us, as to Christ, at baptism, with our choosing to turn away from sin to Christ. Self-denial for the medieval pilgrim involved separation from normal life at home. He would have to make his will, and perhaps even an agreement with his wife as to how long she should wait for him to come home before she could consider herself free to remarry. Because pilgrimage is as much about the inner journey as physical travel, the pilgrim would seek reconciliation with anyone he had wronged, make a sincere confession, and go to Mass. For a time, the pilgrim was casting off all that bound him to his prior existence.

As a result, on his journey the pilgrim entered with Christ into the wilderness, to that threshold between past and future, without any status other than as a pilgrim, without any tie other than to the present journey. Like the great rood, pilgrimage is poised on the threshold between earth and heaven. By leaving behind the ties that bound him in life, the pilgrim put his destiny in God's hand, for God to lead him where he would have him.

Within the pilgrim journey that is our human life, it is often our temptation to try to assert control over our own lives and decide for ourselves where God wants us to be. We may even seek to rebel against God's will for us. This was the response of the prophet Jonah to the Lord's command to go and preach repentance to the people of Nineveh. Jonah tried to journey as far from Nineveh as he could go, until the tempest that God sent convinced him he could not escape. And so he allowed himself to be thrown overboard, to be swallowed by the whale, to be taken where he did not want to go but where God would use him for his work.

In the wilderness Satan tempted Christ to follow Jonah's example and to flee his vocation, but Jesus, with Jonah, chose, as it were, to let himself be flung into the sea. Jesus linked his own death on the cross with the 'sign of Jonah': 'For just as Jonah was three days and three nights in the belly of the sea monster, so for three days and three nights the Son of Man will be in the heart of the earth' (Matt. 12:40). Even as Christ on the cross was prepared to relinquish his life and the medieval pilgrim to cut the ties that bound him, so we as Christians in our own day must, in order to take up the cross, be prepared to lose control and allow the wind of the Holy Spirit to blow us where it wills. To embrace the rood is to enter upon the threshold of we know not what, trusting in the power of the cross to guide us to our destination.

For the earthly pilgrim, that goal was the city of Jerusalem; for every Christian, our hope is in the heavenly Jerusalem, the City of God. As Christians, it is our dichotomous privilege to be citizens both of the human city and of the City of God. We straddle the rood screen in church, with one foot on earth and one in heaven.

If this belonging fully neither to earth nor to heaven is experienced in a solitary way, then that experience can be disorientating. But the great rood and the accompanying screen are emphatic reminders that the Christian's pilgrimage is anything but solitary. The images of Mary and John at the foot of the crucifix, recalling the new relationships of motherhood and sonship that were Christ's gift to them from the cross, were a sign to Christians that they too shared this new intimacy with the whole Christian family, past, present, and future. The Blessed Virgin was also their mother and St John, the beloved disciple, their brother; both were praying for Christians on earth journeying to join them in the heavenly kingdom. On the lowest part of the screen, facing the congregation in the nave, were further images of angels and saints, reminding the people of their fellowship with 'angels and archangels and all the company of heaven'. The whole screen was thus an icon of the heavenly hierarchy and its communion with the Church in pilgrimage on earth. The saints along with the earthly Church stood literally under the cross, sharing with earthly Christians their dependence on Christ's passion. The saints accompanied the pilgrims on their journeys; they were their companions in that peculiar threshold between earth and heaven.

Despite our ever-greater technological capacity to control the mechanisms of life, our world's existence is as precarious as ever. We remain poised between peace and war; technology has increased rather than decreased the gap between rich and poor. We still live with the 'memory' of the Fall, and no amount of our human wealth and intelligence can heal that wound. But the image of the rood reminds us that God in Christ is still reaching out to us to heal us.

Human beings cannot make their way into the future by ignoring the past. Our personal histories of failures and successes, our human history of war and conflict, resolution and accomplishment, all these are written into the fabric of our being and enmeshed into our psyches. When God reaches out to humanity, when he seeks to heal and transform the wounds of history by providing us with a new and living way into his future, he interacts with us in a way that is true to us and to our human nature. In the cross, God confronts us with our archetypal fear – the fear of death. He does not show us the cross, however, in order to terrify us into submission to his will. Rather, the cross is the sign of his victory over death, a sign which he offers us to heal our own fear, to assure us that in Christ the grip of death over humanity has been decisively broken, once for all.

We cannot treat the cross as a thing apart – merely as a fashion statement or simply as an identifying Christian symbol. The great rood reminds us that central to the significance of the cross is its power to connect. It binds us in new relationships across boundaries of blood ties, nationality, colour and gender; it links God's saving revelation of himself in human history, his presence with us here and now, and his future coming in judgement; it joins heaven and earth, God and humanity. The gift of the cross is the gift of God's love for his people, and it opens for us the gate to new and everlasting life within an infinite community of love, peace and justice. Christ in his words to Mary and John from the cross is inviting us, too, to accept his cross and to journey with them and the whole Church – our new mothers and fathers and sisters and brothers – along a way to a new future. When we choose to embrace the cross, the only death we are choosing is death to the sin and hatred and evil which separate our world from God and from his will for us. When we choose to embrace that cross, then we are choosing the life and love that radiate from Christ's victory over death and the grave to the whole human community, past, present, and in the age to come.

I AM A PILGRIM. I WENT ON A JOURNEY throughout the world to see where wisdom and righteousness were to be found.

On my way I found civil war. Peoples who had lived as neighbours for hundreds of years were killing one another, destroying one another's homes. I asked, 'Why are you doing this?' They replied, 'He belongs to a different tribe.' 'Her faith wishes to destroy my faith.' 'They want our land. God gave this place to us.' 'They are terrorists.' 'My friend is his enemy, so he is my enemy too.'

I came to another place. It looked like a rich land, and a few people seemed very wealthy, and they lived behind high walls and gates. But there were many, many more people who lived in desperate poverty. Children were starving on the streets. Also in the streets were soldiers, uniformed, strong, and well armed. I went to one of the big gates and asked, 'Why are things like this?' But there was no reply.

I came to another place. This place also was rich. The land was fertile. The shops groaned with every kind of food and clothing and leisure equipment. Even the poor drove around in cars. Almost everyone seemed to have more than enough. I asked, 'How can you be so rich when there are so many in the world who are so poor?' They replied, 'We have tried to help them. We have loaned them lots of money, but they haven't paid it back yet, so we can't do anything else.' I asked, 'Could the poor find asylum here, then?' 'Oh no, we cannot afford to support them here.'

I came to a lonely wood. In the wood, there was a fence which barred my way so I could go no further. I could not climb it. I could not get to an end to go around. I looked through the fence and saw beyond it to another place, a different kind of place. Where before I had seen hatred and civil war, here I saw a land of peace and harmony. Where before I saw hunger and suffering, here were fertility and plenty. Everyone had more than enough. Here there were no more fences or walls; here there were no soldiers.

I looked up and I saw a man nailed to a tree, hanging there and dying. I wondered why, here on the threshold of a glorious new world, this man was being executed. Was it simply another example of the inhumanity and cruelty of that old world? I asked, 'Why are you there on the tree? What have you done?' He said, 'I am here for love's sake. I am here for love of this cruel world you have seen, for the love of its people.'

I said, 'But this other place, why is it different?' He said, 'Love.' I continued, 'Why is there no want?' 'Love' was his answer. I asked, 'How can I get there?' He bade me look back to the world I had left, to the rich and the poor, the peaceful and the violent, the indifferent and the compassionate. He said, 'See these people. They are your sons and daughters, your sisters and brothers, your mothers and fathers. Love them, and you shall be free.'

5

'Eli, Eli, lama sabachthani? . . . My God, my God, why hast thou forsaken me?' (Matt. 27:46)

TARJEI PARK

The scene could hardly have been more different from Calvary. It was a crystal-clear autumn morning in New York City in the opening year of the twenty-first century. Millions of New Yorkers were beginning their working day. And something happened, something that was to horrify a nation. At 8.46 a.m. a Boeing 767 passenger airliner was flown into the north tower of the World Trade Center. Fifteen minutes later America and millions more people around the world watched live news footage on their television screens of a second 767 flying directly into the south tower. It was a moment simultaneously horrifying and unbelievable. As this second plane ploughed into the tower 10,000 gallons of fuel exploded in a fireball against and within the building. Thousands would die, and the images that were seen over the following hours will never be forgotten by this generation. By the end of the day Manhattan was covered in ash. We had entered the twenty-first century as witnesses to an American tragedy which shook that nation to its core. The personal tragedies of the mourning families were shared profoundly across the USA and the world. Millions watched the scenes as they were televised and re-televised with tears in their eyes. Even in the days following it was impossible for many to look at the newspaper photographs of bodies falling from the towers without wanting to weep.

The reactions to that morning were many and various. Making sense of it was not easy. Here was violence visited on a people who generally thought of themselves as being a good and upright nation, and whose very banknotes expressed their trust in God. More specifically, here was violence visited upon working Americans just starting their day; here was violence visited upon Americans who happened to be making a domestic flight that morning, husbands, wives, fathers, mothers, children. For the citizens of the USA, and, indeed, for many across the world, there was something which made this 'act of war' rather different from others. Again and again came a motif: these victims were innocent.

Now, of course, the victims of 11 September were no *more* innocent than those of Dresden or Hiroshima. Large-scale civilian slaughter was not new and had been practised by most of the powerful nations in the twentieth century. The morning of 11 September was an horrific wake-up call to the reality of how hated the USA was by people who felt that they had been on the receiving end of American violence for quite some time. Yet for the USA and their friends a profound grief was expressed over the 'innocent' victims of 11 September. And there *was* innocence there, heart-breakingly it was there: young children holding the hands of parents on board the planes as they struck the towers. There was such great love too: in all the horror, men and women phoning answer-phones at home to say one last time to their partners and children, 'I love you.'

In the days that followed there were many gestures and acts of solidarity inside and outside the USA. Places of worship were filled to overflowing as mourners lamented and prayed to God. Overwhelmingly trust in God remained. By and large, fists were not shaken at God, but at the demonised organiser of the outrage.

But why not despair of God? Why not believe that God is somehow answerable? Why not cry out 'Why?' to God. Did Jesus not do this on the cross, and in so doing echo the self-same cry made by millions of others across the ages? 'My God, my God, why hast thou forsaken me?'

In the midst of life we are in horror. Yet in the Western world it is often presumed that horror is an intrusive element into ordered community. When horrific and cruel things happen we ask 'Why?' This is particularly true when the seemingly innocent suffer or die. Grief-stricken, we cry out, 'Why?'

Jesus Christ's cry of dereliction on the cross contains within it a painful paradox. For although it is formally a cry for explanation, it is also an affirmation of God and an anguished accusation. It is a recognition that God is still God, but also that God has forsaken the crier to a most sadistic execution. The horrifying reality is that the God of Abraham, Isaac and Jacob, the God who has an everlasting covenant with his chosen, has abandoned a faithful son of that covenant to a degrading, violent death. Furthermore, we must be clear as to what the cry of dereliction is not. It is not a denial of the existence of God, nor is it in itself a rejection of God. It is an affirmation and an accusation in the form of a painful cry for explanation, 'Why?'

The cry of dereliction is an engagement with a pre-existing cry, for it is, of course, the opening cry of the psalmist in Psalm 22. Christ's cry of dereliction from the cross has both the literal, immediate meaning in the suffering of Calvary, and a simultaneous meaning, which is the gesture to the narrative of the psalm. It thus is both particular and general – it connects with moments when human beings have cried the same cry both before, and since. Yet this connecting with the cries of others has sometimes been discouraged, as what happened to Christ on the cross was not 'just' suffering – Christ was bringing about the salvation of the world.

Clearly, what was happening on the cross to Jesus Christ has theological significance and ramifications beyond the moments of perceived abandonment which, however cruel and painful, happen every day to human beings. The christological narratives of atonement, redemption, and salvation by the cross do frame Christ's agonies in such a way as to make them incomparable with the suffering of other innocents. It is not possible to equate everyday horror with what was happening on the cross. It is not theologically permissible. The suffering of Christ has salvific ramifications which other suffering does not, because Jesus on the cross was who he was. The suffering of Christ on the cross was 'once, only once, and once for all'. Yet the cry of dereliction from the cross, the cry for *explanation* from the cross, is a highly charged theological verse of Scripture which has unsettled theologians over the centuries because it seems to question who Jesus was, and is. It seems to question the divine nature of Christ. If Christ is divine, how can divinity abandon him?

It is possible here, as a theological 'shorthand', to apply the christological hymn found in the second chapter of St Paul's Letter to the Philippians:

> Let the same mind be in you that was in Christ Jesus,
> who, though he was in the form of God,
> did not regard equality with God
> as something to be exploited,
> but emptied himself,
> taking the form of a slave,
> being born in human likeness.
> And being found in human form,
> he humbled himself
> and became obedient to the point of death –
> even death on a cross.
> Therefore God also highly exalted him
> and gave him the name
> that is above every name,
> so that at the name of Jesus
> every knee should bend,
> in heaven and on earth and under the earth,
> and every tongue should confess
> that Jesus Christ is Lord,
> to the glory of God the Father (Phil. 2:5–11).

Christ, although 'in the form of God', *empties* himself of divine power. The Greek word here, *kenosis* (emptying), has led theologians to talk of kenotic christology. That is, that those aspects that would have given Christ 'equality with God' are understood as having been emptied as Christ is 'born in human likeness'. Thus the man hanging on the cross does not have some kind of divine potential waiting in reserve which he is deliberately not using. The man hanging on the cross is fully human, having emptied himself of the predicates of divinity, having at the heart of his identity an *absence*.

To the person suffering the cruel agonies that happen to human beings every day, christological doctrine might have little relevance. Even to the person of faith the response might be, 'Who cares about christology!? *Why, God, have you let this happen? Why have you not stood by me?*' And this *is* ultimately what Jesus cries too from the cross, and by using the words of the psalmist, his personal cry has within it the cry as cried by others: 'My God, my God, why hast thou forsaken me?'

There is no emotionally satisfactory answer to these questions when they are asked by people in despair. Talk of non-intervention as being part of the gift of free will is of little consolation, and seems to go against a good many passages from Scripture. There are times when the blunt cruelty of a situation is so overwhelming that our faith in the goodness of God is tested beyond any casual theological speculation. This is movingly conveyed in David Scott's poem 'Dean Tait'. Archibald Tait was Dean of Carlisle, and later Archbishop of Canterbury, and in the space of one month, March 1856, five of his daughters died in an epidemic of scarlet fever.

> Quite put aside were any thoughts
> of the state of the Cathedral roof
> Instead, a quiet agony, waiting
> for the stethoscope's final figure of eight,
> and the click of the doctor's bag.
> He never thought there could be this routine
> to death: the prayer book, the size of his palm;
> his wife, half in doubt because of the fever,
> hiding the sick-room drawings away;
> and at their prayers each day
> in a borrowed house, they tested
> the Bible texts against a silent nursery.[1]

Where is God in all this? What responsibility does God have for it? When appalling cruelty and evil occur these are not idle questions, they are natural questions made by the faithful. The answer to these questions is not necessarily a comfortable one. And conclusions that have been reached can challenge our whole view of who God is.

Elie Wiesel recalls a hauntingly painful event that he experienced as a teenager in Auschwitz. A teacher of Talmud who had befriended Wiesel in the Nazi death camp took him one night back to his own barracks where three rabbis, 'all erudite and pious men', masters of Talmud, Halakhah, and Jewish jurisprudence, decided to put God on trial. They decided in 'a rabbinic court of law to indict the Almighty' for 'allowing His children to be massacred'. Over several nights evidence was presented and then a unanimous verdict was reached: 'the Lord God Almighty, Creator of Heaven and Earth, was found guilty of crimes against creation and humankind.' Wiesel writes, 'I remember: I was there, and I felt like crying. But there nobody cried.' Then, after an 'infinity of silence', one of them looked at the sky and said, 'It's time for evening prayers', and they all recited Maariv, the evening service.[2]

There can be no obvious response to this trial and to the prayerful reaction of those involved. The ambiguity remains powerfully, the God they prayed to *had* been found guilty.

Even to the devoutly faithful it is natural to ask questions relating to *God's* responsibility when appallingly evil events happen. It is sometimes just not acceptable to lay the blame for moral evil on other human beings. And why not blame the Creator for physical evil? If God is a faithful God, what does this mean when there seems little evidence of it? If God *abandons* the faithful to horrific evil, what kind of God is God? Does it indeed make God morally useless?

Again, it offers little consolation to those who suffer such evil, but the default answer to such a question typically relates to the fact that as humans we have free will. That is, if we are truly free, we must be free to live without the 'interference' of God. So God in principle 'abandons' us to make of our lives what we will. But perhaps this is just part of the picture. Perhaps our primary focus should not be on our sense of the *absence* of God, but rather that some of us may have a rather question-able sense of the *presence* of God, or more specifically, the *intervention* of God.

Now, clearly within classical theism, on one level it makes little sense to speak about the absence and presence of God. God by definition is present everywhere. What we can talk about is the *perceived* absence and presence of God, how far God is perceived to be part of a situation or event. We might want to draw a line between a formal theological requirement to assert that God is everywhere present and can never be absent, and the human perception of God's presence and absence, and intervention. Yet such a line has not been so clear in the Judeo-Christian scriptural tradition. In the great historical narratives of the Old Testament God is understood as intervening for Israel, classically in the events of the Passover and escape from Egypt, and God's presence is seen as specifically localised out in the wilderness with Moses and the Israelites. God is also understood to 'hide his face', and this under-standing of *hester panim*, of the hiddenness of the face, reflects the experience of God not being there for us, and we shall return to this experience shortly.

However, in the Old Testament there is also an understanding of the omnipresence of God, that God is always there, beautifully evoked in Psalm 139:

> Where can I go from your spirit?
> Or where can I flee from your presence?
> If I ascend to heaven, you are there;
> if I make my bed in Sheol, you are there.
> If I take the wings of the morning
> and settle at the farthest limits of the sea,
> even there your hand shall lead me,
> and your right hand shall hold me fast (Ps. 139:7–10).

Many faithful people speak readily of the presence of God in their lives, they give testimony to times and places when God has been with them and helped them – has readily intervened. Yet if God is indeed sensed as present in this interventionist way, the sense of his absence at other times is therefore most certainly guaranteed. And when the sense of an interventionist God is further influenced by personal projections, the result can be a very unhelpful misunderstanding of God.

For example, one of the distinctive shifts of emphasis or trends across the Western religious world in the late twentieth and early twenty-first centuries has been an increased interest in 'spirituality'. In the Western world forms of practice which centre on *experiential* approaches to God or to things 'spiritual' have become very popular.

Much of this has taken place outside traditional church structures. Indeed, much of this interest is distinctly unstructured. 'Spirituality' is seen by many as an intensely individual aspect. It is, perhaps, an individ- ualistic space in which personal identity is a defining factor. 'Spirituality' is about an individual's experience of God or, very commonly, a spiritual realm, a realm that is often that individual's 'personal space'. The great danger in this understanding of spirituality is that God is seen from a self-interested perspective. The God who is perceived is often a God with all kinds of projected attributes that derive from a self-interested unrelated self. God is not the 'hidden God', but a God who is revealed to the individual. God is individually present, or perhaps, a very heavily projected God is present.

The 'problem' occurs when this sense of presence is not just presence but intervention. Claims of a sense of the presence of God can find expres- sion in all kinds of attributes given to God, but claims of God intervening take us into further problematic areas both theologically and ethically, quite simply because God does not intervene in the way in which many people assume. We cannot say that a particular event was down to an individual act of intervention by God, as it would make God sadistically selective. Why is one child healed and not another – however faithful they, their family and friends may be? Why is the faithful airline pilot not given some intuition that tragedy will befall a particular flight? Yet the belief that God actively intervenes in events and lives persists. And this is where christology comes back – God's inter- vention is not about halting or reversing consequences in life, but it is about presence without manipulation, it is about the absence of power. And this finds expression in Christ hanging on the cross. Divinity in humanity, empty of manipulative power, but carrying the cruelty of the world.

The incarnate Son of God is, in who he is, the greatest example of divine intervention. The birth and human life of Jesus Christ are God intervening in human history. But the incarnation is about intervention and also self-gift. It is about being so fully present to humanity that divinity is emptied. Humanity is embraced, and transcendent powers are laid aside in a life of self-offering – self-offering which leads to the horror of the undeserved human violence of the cross.

Yet powerfully the crucifixion, and particularly the cry of abandonment, are, among many things, the exemplar for a mature 'spirituality'. Spirituality which finds expression in gushing affirmations of how God intervenes for a person every day in various events is often delusional and misguided, and can bring great bitterness and pain when at some cruel point God does not 'intervene'. The realisation that God is not going to live your life for you, so to speak, is not a loss of belief in God, but is the recognition of who God is and who we are. To live on earth is to live as people abandoned to our own brokenness, our own fallen-ness. We should not assume that order and civility should prevail, because chaotic cruelty and horror are as much the nature of reality as are occasions of goodness and love. When good and lovely things happen in life they are extras, gifts – glimpses into what we can achieve when *we* incarnate God's will.

Emmanuel Lévinas writes the following:

> What is the meaning of the suffering of innocents? Does it not prove a world without God, an earth on which man is the only measure of good and evil? The simplest and most common reaction would be to decide for atheism. This would also be the reasonable reaction of all those whose idea of God until that point was of some kindergarten deity who distributed prizes, applied penalties, or forgave faults and in His goodness treated men as eternal children. But I have to ask these people: With what kind of underendowed demon, what kind of magician did they people their heaven, if they now declare that this heaven is empty? And why are they still searching, under this empty heaven, for a world that is rational and good?[3]

Immature understandings of God which involve indulgent parental fantasies are not going to bring us closer to God but further away. Lévinas wrote the above upon reading what purported to be a text which had been found preserved in a bottle in the ruins of the Warsaw Ghetto, concealed amongst charred stone and human bones. A man by the name of Yosl Rakover is one of the last survivors of the ghetto, but aware that he will soon be killed as artillery fire and shells are exploding and shattering the walls of the houses round about him. He has lost his wife and six children in the horrors of the ghetto, all in the most terrible cruelty – one daughter, Rachel, ten years old, is driven by starvation to escape at night out of the ghetto with a friend in order to search for bread in the city garbage cans. She is discovered by the Nazi sentries and their Polish helpers, who pursue her. She attempts to run, but her weakness causes her to collapse, and 'the Nazis drove holes through her skull.' In his letter Yosl Rakover decides to call God to account. Why has God abandoned his people to the evils of the Nazis, the violence, disease and starvation of the ghetto? And he ends his letter in the following way:

> I have followed Him, even when He pushed me away. I have obeyed His commandments, even when He scourged me for it. I have loved Him, I have been in love with Him and remained so, even when He made me lower than the dust, tormented me to death, abandoned me to shame and mockery.
>
> . . . Here, then, are my last words to You, my angry God: None of this will avail You in the least! You have done everything to make me lose my faith in You, to make me cease to believe in You. But I die exactly as I have lived, an unshakeable believer in You.
>
> Praised be forever the God of the dead, the God of vengeance, of truth and judgement, who will soon unveil His face to the world again and shake its foundations with His mighty voice.
>
> 'Sh'ma Yisroel! Hear, Israel! The Lord is our God, the Lord is one. Into Your hands, O Lord, I commend my soul.'[4]

This is the heart of the matter: to affirm God even when God's hiddenness is at its most real. There is this in the now famous lines found inscribed on a cellar wall in Cologne where some Jews had hidden for the entire duration of the war:

> I believe in the sun, even when it doesn't shine.
> I believe in love, even when I don't feel it.
> I believe in God, even when He is silent.

The concept of the hiddenness of God is not new; it is not some modern or post-modern response to problems with theism. It is a profoundly scriptural understanding of God; a God who sometimes 'hides the face', hester panim. Towards the end of the Book of Deuteronomy we read, 'The Lord . . . spurned his sons and daughters. He said: I will hide my face from them' (32:19–20), and in the Book

of the Prophet Isaiah we read, 'Truly, you are a God who hides himself,
O God of Israel, the Saviour' (45:15).

These understandings of the hiddenness of God stem from the
human experience of the absence of God. They stem from the human
inability at times to experience the presence of God. In classical theism
God cannot be absent, because God is omnipresent. Yet the localised sense
of the presence and, importantly, the absence of God is scripturally
attested. The question 'Where is God in all this suffering?' is rather
a way of saying 'I cannot sense that God is present when all this
suffering happens.'

To perceive that God is 'hidden' in this sense is not necessarily
indicative of spiritual short-sightedness, but is perhaps a mature recognition of what we can know and experience of God. The God who is
easily experienced is perhaps not really there.

This is not to say that all experience of God is delusional, but that
discernment of our experience and understanding of the presence of
God is essential. Without discernment indulgent fantasies easily develop
and further delusion is never far behind.

Much of this can relate to our experience of God outside any
experience of suffering. In Christian theology the notion of the hidden
God, *Deus absconditus*, has been an important premise that has had the
very necessary function of making sure that God is not completely
domesticated and personalised by human psychological needs. There is
always that of God which transcends human understanding; that of
God which is hidden. And there are times when God seems to be fully
hidden, and is perceived to be 'absent'.

So the perceived absence of God is as much an issue in good times
as in bad. But it is perhaps when we are at cruel and painful emotional extremes, that the sense of God's absence, of the lack of intervention,
is most acutely experienced.

So where do we go from here? Where does Christ's cry of dereliction from the cross leave us? Or, rather, where does it take us? It
takes us to a bleak place, a place of absence. It takes us to a place of
cruel punishment. It takes us to a place where we have seemingly been
abandoned by our closest human companions and by God. In
Matthew's Gospel 'My God, my God, why hast thou forsaken me?'
are the only words spoken by Christ from the cross; Christ's summary

vocalisation of his suffering is his sense that God has abandoned him.

This should lead us to acknowledge that such a sense of abandonment is not a dangerous or erroneous sense – Jesus had it. Jesus, emptied of the predicates of God, truly human, knows that sense of abandonment and cries out that very human cry. But the dereliction of the cross is not the end of the story.

Jesus Christ suffered as a human being, and that human experience is taken up into divinity. We should not see this as a theological problem over how limited human perception can supplement unlimited divine perception. But the Christian mystery is surely this: that *crucified* humanity is taken up into divinity.

There is no evil which can separate us from Jesus Christ. Christ in his humanity was one of us, and in his humanity he experienced the human suffering and the dereliction of the cross. He experienced the sense of cruel abandonment, of God 'hiding his face', as he died. But Jesus was not abandoned ultimately; and no, that dark and desolate Friday afternoon is not the end of the story, because through Jesus Christ's risen and ascended crucified brokenness God searches out the broken of this world with the hope of new life. We could perhaps say that God 'intervenes' through the broken and healed humanity of Christ. And we could perhaps go further here and say that God 'intervenes' through all human beings who incarnate the will of God.

We could say that on a clear September morning in New York City in 2001 the love and goodness of God permeated the hearts and minds of members of the New York City Fire Department. As some were running towards the entrance to the tower they had to avoid being struck down by falling bodies slamming into the plaza around them; they were running through a twenty-first-century vision of hell. Hundreds of Fire Department members died in the tragedy. We could say that such deaths are a known risk in the work they do. But few observers could fail to be moved by the dedication of the Fire Department that morning to saving whoever they could in that hell. There was something of *sacrifice* about their deaths. And it is not an unjustified superimposition to see something of the divine will in their saving work on 11 September; a solidarity with humanity in hell.

Oh, where have you been, my blue-eyed son?
Oh, where have you been, my darling young one?
I met a young woman whose body was burning
And it's a hard rain's a-gonna fall.[5]

HELL ON EARTH IS A REALITY. THERE ARE occasions in life that are so crushingly evil. There are sights seen that just should not be seen. There are extremes of cruelty that are just not acceptable. There are times of such sadness that they break your heart. There are places we just should not have to be.

Is it all redeemable?

He 'was crucified, dead, and buried: He descended into hell.'

What was Jesus doing in hell? He was looking for his friend Judas Iscariot. Judas had done something so wrong that he could not forgive himself, and feeling incapable of being forgiven, in bitter tears of regret, he hanged himself. Well, Jesus went looking for him, and in hell he found him. He walked over to him, kissed him, and took his hand.

Miracles occur in hell.

When we see images on the television or in magazines and books it is often evil visited on children that makes us cry: the girl on the pavement in the Warsaw ghetto holding her starved little sister, the Vietnamese girl burning with napalm running from her village, the terrified boy in Gaza tucked up against his father, crying before he is shot. And these really are moments of hell on earth.

Loveliness happens too.

I remember seeing a brother and sister on the television news. He was about eight and she was about four. They had become separated from their family following the dreadful flooding in Mozambique in the spring of 2000; their family might not even be alive. They had managed to get a bag of maize meal from one of the relief camps, but they were not going to open it – it was to be a present for their parents when they found them. After talking to the news correspondent they ran off together to continue the search for their family. The boy was so caring of his sister. The love and responsibility of these two poor children was just heart-achingly beautiful.

Jésus le Christ, lumière intérieure,
ne laisse pas mes ténèbres me parler.
Jésus le Christ, lumière intérieure,
donne-moi d'accueillir ton amour.

Lord Jesus Christ, your light shines within us.
Let not my doubts nor my darkness speak to me.
Lord Jesus Christ, your light shines within us.
Let my heart always welcome your love.[6]

6

'I thirst' (John 19:28)

SABINA ALKIRE

'Our charism is to satiate the thirst of Jesus for love and souls – by working at the salvation and sanctification of the poorest of the poor.'[1] Responding to this last word of Christ is the public purpose of Mother Teresa's sisters and brothers, the heart of the calling to serve the poor that she received on her train journey to Darjeeling, and the spiritual focus of her community now that she is gone. Every convent chapel of the Missionaries of Charity throughout the world, whether active or contemplative, has a bloody crucifix and by it – always – two words: 'I thirst.' They are generally pasted up in paper letters, that arc slightly away from the wall at the tips. And most visitors come and go without noticing the saying. If they glimpse it at all, they rarely grasp its significance.

But the phrase is highly significant. The fifth last word – 'I am thirsting' (in the present continuous tense) – represents to this community an insight that gives a sure-footed joy to their work, an insight that deserves to be shared, although without the usual romance with which journalists paint these sisters in blue-rimmed saris.

The insight is not self-evident, for the text 'I thirst' is remarkably ambiguous. Is this the straightforward utterance of a man dying in extreme dehydration? Does it refer to Psalm 69? 'I am weary with my crying; my throat is parched. My eyes grow dim with waiting for my God . . . They gave me poison for food, and for my thirst they gave me vinegar to drink' (3:21). Does it express Jesus' willingness, and even eagerness, now to drink the cup he had earlier prayed God would lift from his lips? Does it relate in some way to the thirst of God for the souls of the faithful? The one text is susceptible to multiple interpretations. And the sisters do not articulate their own interpretation at length, which is why it might better be called an insight, a way of seeing into a situation and allowing it to affect one.

Their insight is that the thirst of Christ on the cross and the thirst of Christ in the living poor are one and the same. Towards the end of Matthew's Gospel Jesus tells a story of judgement, where the Son of Man separates the sheep from the goats, and the chosen query: 'Lord, when was it that we saw you hungry and gave you food, or thirsty and gave you drink? And when was it that we saw you a stranger and welcomed you or naked and gave you clothing? And when was it that we saw you sick or in prison and visited you?' (25:37–39).

Here, too, is an image of a thirsting Lord.

The image of a thirsting Lord leads to a different way of hearing the word of Christ on the cross. Sometimes when we ponder the words 'I thirst' we consider the painful dehydration of a body that had been up to 18 hours without water, that had lost blood through the scourging by leather laced with bone shards and the crown of thorns, and is now hung in the sun. So we realise with a start that in these alone of the seven last words Jesus spoke of himself – his own physical agony – which we may not have realised so acutely before. We begin to grasp that Jesus suffered. Sometimes when we ponder 'I thirst' we see how central this utterance, this lone expression of bodily need, was to the doctrinal jigsaw puzzle the early Church tried to assemble: How did the fragile human body of the person of Jesus fit together with his divinity? And so we probe the mystery of the incarnation – of God made flesh.

However we appreciate this utterance, whether through sharpened imagination or through a historical entrée into the controversies of the early Church, we tend to consider it in the past. In contrast, Mother Teresa's sisters and brothers hear the words in the present. They hear 'I thirst' in the stumpy limbs of the leper, in the slumped shoulders of the depressed and unloved, in the watchful eyes of the AIDS patient, the lilting voice of the orphan, and the rasp of the dying. The insight, the recognition that gives rise to action, is that these words are true for God in the present. Christ is present in those that suffer.

> Jesus makes Himself the hungry one, the naked one, the homeless one, the unwanted one, and He says, 'You did it to Me.' On the last day He will say to those on His right, 'Whatever you did to the least of these you did to Me', and He will also say to those on His left, 'Whatever you neglected to do for the least of these you neglected to do it for Me.'[2]

This insight firmly and explicitly links the two passages. As Mother Teresa put it in a letter to her community, '"I Thirst" and "You did it to me" – Remember always to connect the two.'[3]

Such a spirituality of thirst has a proactive aspect both towards the poor and also towards God. For by their acts of love and service, Christians hope to quench the thirst of God. In the last letter of her life, Mother Teresa wrote, 'Let our gratitude be our strong resolution to quench the Thirst of Jesus by lives of real charity – love for Jesus in prayer, love for Jesus in our Sisters, love for Jesus in the poorest of the poor – nothing else.'[4]

Some might claim that such words border on heresy, because they seem to attribute to God a fundamental 'need' for human works and overestimate the importance of any human effort. A resolution to quench Jesus' thirst might seem overly earnest or arrogantly self-important. But many others articulate a similar resolution to act on God's behalf. Teresa of Avila approached it when she wrote, 'Christ has no body now on earth but yours, no hands but yours, no feet but yours; yours are the eyes through which to look at Christ's compassion to the world.' And Dag Hammerskjöld wrote, 'If you fail, it is God who, through your betrayal of Him, will fail Mankind. You imagine that you can bear the responsibility to God; can you bear it for Him?'[5] Taken in isolation, each of these statements attributes more to human efforts than they deserve or can bear. But framed within an understanding of God as the one who calls a people into union with the divine will, who fructifies their efforts, who strives for justice even when it is thwarted, and who will ultimately overcome evil regardless of human failures, these statements catalyse responsible action.

Hearing 'I thirst' in this way unleashes love. Compare, if you would, in your mind's eye, a standard government leprosy clinic with one whose workers are permeated by the insight above. What differs between them is not the treatment. In both, let us imagine, the patients have similarly good, if simple, sanitation; they have similarly good, if basic, medication. In both they have simple food, and they learn how to adjust to their condition. The difference is not in the treatment; the real difference is the intangible love and joy that surely infiltrates the one whose staff are first and foremost 'contemplatives in the heart of the world', to quote Mother Teresa. These active contemplatives begin the day with Francis' prayer, 'Lord, make me a channel of your peace, that where there is hatred, I may bring love . . .' Their prayers include vivid expressions of hope, such as the words of John Henry Newman:

> Let us preach You without preaching;
> not by words but by our example;
> by the catching force, the sympathetic influence of what we do,
> the evident fullness of the love our hearts bear to You.

What is important is not the words of the prayers nor their setting (in simple chapels in front of the peeling black paper letters, 'I thirst'). What is important is that spiritual disciplines such as these form the sisters into what William Blake might have called steady 'beams of love'.[6] How the intangible love and joy is expressed may vary – from running feet and smiles to a steadiness of purpose. But it is this love alone that distinguishes 'Christian' from 'government' clinics.

If we are to understand this last word of Jesus as being God's presence in the poor, it is obvious that we will be drawn somehow, each Christian according to his or her own vocation, but each Christian without exception, to address the poor. This is not, of course, a remotely revolutionary conclusion. When James, Cephas and John 'perceived the grace' that was in the apostle Paul and accepted his and Barnabas' mission to the Gentiles, they reportedly laid down but one condition for that mission (according to Paul): to 'remember the poor' (Gal. 2:10). The letter of James upbraids readers who are biased towards the well-dressed rich, rather than being partial to the poor (Jas. 2:5–9), and the first letter of John asks, 'How does God's love abide in anyone who has the world's goods and sees a brother or sister in need and yet refuses to help?' (3:17). When Christianity became established in Alexandria in the second century, Clement of Alexandria, who cared for the souls of wealthy Alexandrians, wrote a treatise with the blunt title, *Who then is the rich man that shall be saved?* In the mid-second century Bishop Polycarp, who taught Irenaus (and may have sat at the feet of the apostle John), wrote concern for the poor into the presbyter's job description: 'And let the presbyters be compassionate and merciful to all, bringing back those that wander, visiting all the sick, and not neglecting the widow, the orphan, or the poor.'[7] Whether it was the sermons of St Augustine in Africa, the Councils of the early Church, the journals of mission priests in the New World, liberation theology's 'option for the poor', or the social teachings from *Rerum Novarum* (the Roman Catholic Church's first encyclical on social justice[8]) to *Centisimus Anni* (its most recent), the duty to care for the poor has surfaced habitually. Christianity has the poor in view.

But who are 'the least of our brothers and sisters'? It is hard for those of us who perch at one point on a planet overloaded with information, to take in what is going on around us. Perhaps we might consider a series of 'aerial photos', if you will, describing recent aspects of poverty.

Our planet houses just over six billion people. Of these, one in seven of us are malnourished, according to the Food and Agricultural Organisation.[9] The World Health Organisation tells us that one in six of us do not have clean water to drink.[10] World Bank statistics show that one in five of us live on less than one US dollar a day. Well over one in three of us do not have basic sanitation. Nearly half of us live on less than $2 a day.[11] As the United Nations Development Program pointed out, if the poorest third of the world pooled their income it would not be enough to pay the bill of military expenditure worldwide.[12] If we divided the population of the world into representative groups of five people, the richest person of the five would consume 86 times what the poorest person of the five consumed. If we asked the population of the world to sit down in representative groups of four people, three out of the four members of each group would be from a developing country.[13] If we were then to feed ourselves, the three people from developing countries would get one piece of toast each, while the person from the developed country would get seven pieces of toast – every day, every meal. If there were 60 technological gadgets to distribute, the three developing-country group members would get one each; the fourth person would collect the remaining 57. If we converted all energy units into batteries, the three persons would use one battery each; the fourth person would use up 17 batteries in the same amount of time.[14] We could go on . . .

The obvious thing to do in the face of such inequality is to share, and we do – a little. If the wealthy person of the group had $1000 and was American, he or she would give the other three $1 in total 'foreign aid'; if the person were British it would be $3. If the person were Norwegian it would be $9; if Danish it would be $10. No representative person on the planet gives more.[15] On average throughout all of the groups, the three developing-country members would get $2.20 between them in foreign aid, and the fourth member would retain $997.80, out of which he or she would give another 30 cents as a private donation, retaining $997.50.

Of course, those who are poor are not spread evenly across the world. Three quarters of the people who have less than $1 a day live in Asia (18 per cent live in Africa, and five per cent in Latin America). In South Asia, four out of ten persons are income poor and four out of ten adults are illiterate. In Africa it is five out of ten who are income poor; four out of ten adults are illiterate. Everywhere else less than two in ten are income poor.[16]

When a mother has a baby in Singapore or the United Kingdom or another well-off country, that baby could expect to live to be about 77 years old. When a mother gives birth in Senegal or Haiti or Laos, she can expect her child to die 25 years earlier, at the age of 52.[17] In Sierra Leone the children can expect to live only half as long as Singaporean or British children. In 38 countries the children born today are expected to live a *shorter* life than the children who were born in those countries a decade ago.[18] The fall in life expectancy is even more unjust because the worldwide average life expectancy has risen by four months each year since 1970. We have more food on the planet per person than ever before (and more than enough to feed everyone well), more children in school, and more adults who can read. But still we do not take care of one another.

On 11 September 2001, more than twice as many people on earth died of AIDS than in the tragic catastrophes at the World Trade Center, the Pentagon, and the Pennsylvania airline crash combined. But not only on 11 September. On 10 September and 12 September, and each day that year, an average of 8,219 people died of AIDS and 15,000 contracted HIV/AIDS for the first time.[19]

Spiritual poverty is a less measurable anguish, yet in the last 45 years suicide rates have increased by 60 per cent worldwide. Suicide is now among the three leading causes of death among men and women aged 15–44, and for each suicide there are 20 attempted suicides.[20] In the United States, there are 1.5 times more suicides than homicides.[21] In the UK and Ireland, there is one suicide every 79 minutes. Loneliness and depression, stress, crime, discrimination, and mental illness affect even the materially well off.

One final number is necessary. About one in three persons on the globe self-identifies their religious affiliation as Christian. *That is two billion people!* These are people who walk the corridors of power, people who live on the margins of society, and people in all walks of life in between. Not all of us are destitute. It has been estimated by Ron Sider that Christians command one quarter of world income, or over ten trillion US dollars a year.[22] The faith has been around, and the Church (which is obviously drawn to the poor) has been active throughout the evolutions that created this profile of poverty and wealth. Christianity is the dominant religious affiliation among the people with 7 pieces of toast and 57 gadgets and 17 used-up batteries. And yet there is so much poverty. Gandhi is often cited as saying, 'If Christians lived out their faith fully there would be no Hindus left in India.' It might not be terribly awry to muse that 'If Christians had lived out their faith fully there would not be such poverty on earth.'

How do we apply the same energetic love and spiritual depth that Mother Teresa's sisters show, to such a litany of poverties? Clearly, we see now that addressing 'the least of these my brothers and sisters' requires two approaches. One is to care for the immediate needs of the aged, the lepers, the addicts, the orphaned children, those dying of AIDS, those whom society deems insane. But that alone is not and will never be enough. The other approach is to care by addressing structural issues. As the American civil rights activist Martin Luther King Jr wrote:

> we are called to play the good Samaritan on life's roadside; but that will be only an initial act. One day we must come to see that the whole Jericho road must be transformed so that men and women will not be constantly beaten and robbed as they make their journey on life's highway. True compassion is more than flinging a coin to a beggar; it is not haphazard and superficial. It comes to see that an edifice which produces beggars needs restructuring.[23]

This 'transformation' approach would work doggedly to prevent economic collapse and famine and epidemics before they arise. It would work alongside ethnic minorities who are tired of being splashed by passing cars and served with abuse and not respect. And it would 'let the oppressed go free'. The approach aims to empower the oppressed to help themselves.

Once one moves into these realms of responsibility there are many elements to remember. One must recall that the poor, like anyone else, are created for freedom. We all find life in part by creatively compiling a life among the possibilities that lie open to us – not by living out someone else's dream. We all, including the poor, have different gifts and different tastes: some may select voluntary poverty in order to enjoy a depth of spiritual purity; others are artists for whom aesthetics is an overarching framework; others find God and exercise their gifts in relationships, in good health, in meaningful work, in intellectual pursuits, in religious endeavours. And each of us is only somewhat consistent, somewhat disciplined, somewhat faithful. Finally in order to be responsible and build up structures of justice, we must think through many different implications of any significant initiative – its efficiency, its sustainability, its coherence with other initiatives that are in place, who benefits and who is left out, how the community is affected, and so on.

At the same time ethics must be applied to our analysis, for it teaches us to identify and consider carefully the various and often complex ingredients of a situation. For example, we value and pursue many different good aspects of human life for ourselves and others: life itself (health, security, reproduction), knowledge and beauty, relationships, work and play, practical reason, self-integration, religion. Furthermore, our 'glorious liberty' as children of God means that there are manifold ways to do good and to be good in deep and consistent ways.

A principle of morality such as the love command[24] may usefully apply to human institutions – legal institutions, political institutions, economic institutions – which exist, or should exist, not as ends in themselves, but as means whereby human communities address their own poverties and flourish in plural ways. Whether we are individuals or institutions, we need to specify this principle further; we need a set of more specific considerations (like efficiency, non-discrimination, coherence, duration, fairness, well-roundedness, unintended side-effects, etc) that people can use as a checklist. If a group sits down and takes a plan – such as setting up a string of charter Church schools in a poor province – through all of these considerations, then it will emerge with a clearer understanding of the strengths and oversights of the proposal. Such ethical analysis, however tedious, sensitizes people to the moral considerations of their proposed initiative. For if the goal is transformation in the complexity of human institutions, then disciplined consideration is a necessary complement to prayer.

A well-known and recent example of Christians uniting to face the structural roots of deprivation is the Jubilee 2000 campaign, which has involved 24 million people, including churches, the Pope, the US Congress, researchers, protesters, printers, international institutions and national governments (including that of the UK). The campaign arose because passionless, perfunctory, financial transactions – the repaying of a debt – scarred and broke the lives of 'the least of these my brothers and sisters'. In the words of one of Jubilee 2000's own documents, 'Zambia – where life expectancy will shortly fall to 33 years – will still pay more on debt service than on health and education combined.' The campaign, which united prayer vigils and dramatic social agitation, had a potent effect. The effect was slower than desired, and fragile, but very clearly catalytic. Not only did the Jubilee 2000 campaign catalyse debt relief; it also catalysed the World Bank, bilateral donors, the United Nations, and national governments to collaborate with one another and address poverty systemically, to the best of their joint abilities.[25] What we come back to is that some Christians rightly take a different approach to the poor, and that approach is more professional, more structural, more confrontational, more strategic, more long term. The magnitude and shape of poverty requires it.

But somehow, the angry outburst of a complainant against intellectual property rights or trade regimes on television does not seem to evoke the same compassion as a skeletal figure on a distant street corner. The daily routine of memos and speeches, of staff meetings and scantily skimmed policy reports, is a far cry from the daily rhythm of washing clothes, bathing, feeding, playing, and befriending the poor. The privilege of meeting Christ in the 'distressing disguise of the poor' – which can itself be a religious experience – simply may not occur. Those who work for justice – for changes of policy or structure – may be thrice removed from the faces of those they serve, and may not know the results of their actions (for good or ill). And so often their actions seem tainted with compromise, compliant with the status quo; pushy, naïve, or far-fetched. Furthermore, their actions may seem suspect to companions in faith. The experience of Archbishop Helder Camara is often cited precisely because it is often encountered: 'When I feed the poor, they call me a saint; when I ask why they are poor, they call me a communist.'

It would be easy – so easy – to try to address structures of injustice armed with facts and considerations alone, striking out in anger or enthusiasm, yet leaving off the roots of prayer and Christian community. But what would it be, to be a 'contemplative in the heart of the world' while working for structural change? What would it be to attend to the thirst of Christ in the legislative assemblies or research institutes or executive offices? How does love – the love that distinguished Mother Teresa's clinic from the government's – work in secular structural settings?

Mother Teresa simply did not think it was possible to apply such purity of love to structural change. She said, 'I won't mix in politics . . . I don't involve myself, that's all. If I get stuck in politics, I will stop loving. Because I will have to stand by one, not by all. This is the difference.'[26] One salutes her candour and self-honesty. And she obviously found the work she was to do.

Yet one wonders what might be done by those who strive for justice when they have the same habit of prayer and attentiveness and consideration as religious communities. John of the Cross certainly thought that the Church would be better off when he wrote:

> Those who are very active and think that they are going to encircle the earth with their preaching . . . should realize that they would do the Church much more good, and please God much more . . . if they spent even half of this time being with God in prayer (even though they may not have reached as high a level as this). In this way they would certainly achieve more with less trouble, in one work than they would have done in a thousand: their prayer would merit it and would give them inner strength.[27]

Similarly Dag Hammerskjöld, the visionary leader of the United Nations, recognised the need to root his professional work in silence. He wrote, 'How can you expect to keep your powers of hearing when you never want to listen? That God should have time for you, you seem to take as much for granted as that you cannot have time for Him.' And he dedicated the United Nations' Meditation Room, where delegates and the public alike visit, because, 'We all have within us a center of stillness surrounded by silence.'[28] Many other institutions have done likewise. Even the World Bank has, within a second basement's fluorescent cubicles, an inauspicious meditation room containing miscellaneous prayer carpets and donated artwork. Staff can retreat, take off their shoes, and be still.

Rooms for silence, however essential, are not sufficient. We may rightly decry our own lukewarmness in the past, and the extent to which we were satisfied by a very partial linkage between Christian social justice and secular institutions, and did not think through ethical issues. We may recognise in the ongoing destitution itself that something in our prayer has been awry; it has not discerned the thirst of Christ in the poor, nor grasped the wisdom of God calling out to us from street corners. Yet this creates a rather exciting situation. The Church actually has new ground to break, spiritually and socially, in addressing Christ's thirst among 'the least of these my brothers and sisters'.

John of the Cross proposed that one should approach these situations with a particular combination of utter awe and persistent curiosity:

> You honour God greatly and indeed come near to him, when you
> hold him to be nobler and deeper than anything you can attain. So
> do not settle down or try to find a corner in what your mind and
> heart can grasp . . . And do not be like many heartless people who
> have a low opinion of God: they think that when they cannot
> understand him or sense or feel him, he is further away – when
> the truth is more the opposite: it is when you understand him less
> clearly that you are coming closer to him . . . So you do well at all
> times, whether life, or faith, is smooth, or hard, you do well to
> hold God as hidden, and so to cry out to him, 'Where have you
> hidden?'[29]

It might seem that John describes, at the very least, a hypothesis worth
testing. The confidence or faith he describes is sure: God is hidden
within the situation as surely as a figure in a child's book hides in
the trees and grasses to be discovered. It is God's identity and God's
wisdom that is sought and that is there to be perceived, even if it
cannot be fully understood. If we daily bring whatever work situation,
whatever political dilemma, whatever Gordian knot has arisen, and ask
of God in all openness, 'Where have you hidden?', perhaps we will
learn what we have not yet learnt. We may see the presence of God
fused with the identity of the destitute, as the Missionaries of Charity
do. But we may also perceive the divine hidden in a patient, attentive
analysis or in a bold decision, or in manifold other ways. There is new
ground to break if we are to respond to the ongoing thirst of Christ.

OUR PLANET HOUSES JUST OVER SIX BILLION PEOPLE.
Of these, one in seven of us is malnourished.
One in six of us does not have clean water to drink.
One in five of us lives on less than $1 a day.

The numbers are dry; they do not have voices. The numbers are anonymous; they do not have faces.

Can you listen to this, my sister, and take it in?
Can you sit with us, my brother – just sit with us. Do not be afraid.

Were you to sit with us you'd find that we are not only hungry – you will find that we are funny; we are moody; we have our quirks; we are far more like your friends than you expect. Were you to get to know us you might forget we were hungry and think of us by our names.

We are, still, hungry – we are not statistics; we are people with favourite outfits and hopes and jokes and generosity and joy and quiet disappointment – but it so happens that we hunger.

Can you hold us – our full reality? Can you read the stories of pain and not be overwhelmed? Can you hear of crises and not become embittered? Can you listen to those who seek to transform our world – and who look to your support – and not be cynical?

Sit beside us; just sit beside us.

If you were to sit with us you might marvel at our faith, or at our resilience. Then too, you might withdraw in silence. God, where are you hidden? God . . .?

And God – Love – seems silent; seems powerless. Powerless like Jesus who hung on the cross, thirsting.

> Christ has no body now on earth but yours;
> no hands but yours, no feet but yours...

As you listen to us, my sister, as you think of us, my brother, consider prayer-fully what you can do – with your professional skills and other gifts, with your time, even your emails. How might these respond to the thirst of God; how might they be part of God's work on this planet? Ask these things of God. And the God who thirsts for your love and mine, this God will guide the way you walk.

7

'It is finished' (John 19:30)

It is finished; but not merely ended. *Tetelestai* is the Greek – things have reached their *telos* – their conclusion, but also their goal; it is fulfilled, it is accomplished. But what exactly has been accomplished and how? A victory for God, yes; human salvation and liberation, yes. But what does it mean that it is the crucifixion which brings these things about? And what is our response to be; how are we to *feel* about this finish, this accomplishment?

In the darkness of Good Friday a man watches; a light stands at the gate of Hell. As he watches, two ladies approach, the one meek of aspect, the other stern; they are God's daughters, Mercy and Truth. Mercy says that the light will dazzle the devil and that humankind in Hell will be saved from the powers of darkness. Truth tells her to stop talking nonsense – there's no salvation for human beings: didn't Job say that there is no redemption in Hell? The man sees Mercy and Truth joined by their sisters Peace and Righteousness. He hears Peace echo Mercy's claims and he hears too how Righteousness scoffs at her: 'What! are you raving, or are you dead drunk?' For the Fall, says Righteousness, means that Adam and Eve and all their descendants will dwell in perpetual pain. The man and we wait for the action to unfold and the dispute to be settled.

The man is the fourteenth-century poet William Langland. What he sees here and what follows form the climax of his long poem about society and salvation, *Piers Plowman*.[1] That climax is a poetic treatise on the atonement, the reconciliation of man to God through the cross of Christ. Langland's allegorical stand-off between Mercy and Peace and Truth and Righteousness represents the conflict, apparent at least, between God's love and his justice. God loves his sinning creation and wishes its salvation; yet justice requires that sin be not simply ignored. How can the demands of divine justice and the divine desire for human salvation both together be satisfied? How are human beings justly to be saved? Answers to such questions are sometimes implicit in familiar forms of words in Christian liturgy and hymnody – 'A full, perfect, and sufficient sacrifice, oblation, and satisfaction, for the sins of the whole world'; 'We plead with confidence his sacrifice made once for all upon the cross'; 'There was no other good enough / to pay the price of sin'; 'Just as I am, without one plea / but that thy blood was shed for me.' The familiarity of a given formulation may incline us to overlook how it embodies a particular understanding of the atonement, taken from what is a wide range of different opinions among Christian thinkers as to *how* the cross reconciles human beings to God. The familiarity, indeed, may incline us to accept unquestioningly the understanding offered. But we need to ask questions, not to satisfy an academic fastidiousness, but because what we make of the atonement, how we understand it, how we feel it, will shape our view of God, our sense of ourselves before God, and our soul's relationship with God. Langland understands and feels things very differently from another great religious writer, Milton. A comparison between these poets of past ages allows us to see and to feel something of the range of difference possible over the atonement and to appreciate how much is at stake in the differences. It helps to focus the choices we nowadays may need to make.

In Milton's *Paradise Lost*,[2] the Divine will is that human beings, or at any rate God's elect, should be saved, for the Father's glory shall excel both in mercy and justice, 'but mercy first and last shall brightest shine.' The Father tells us this himself.[3] Yet what permits the effulgence of mercy is the operation of justice; for Milton the immediate point of the crucifixion is to achieve justice. In the end, of course, the purposes of love are served, but Milton's atonement is first and foremost a matter of satisfying the demands of God's justice. The human race is doomed by the Fall and God the Father stands firmly by the condemnation of humankind to death:

> man disobeying,
> Disloyal breaks his fealty, and sins
> Against the high supremacy of heaven,
> Affecting Godhead, and so losing all,
> To expiate his treason hath naught left,
> But to destruction sacred and devote,
> He with his whole posterity must die. (3. 203–9)

This concern for justice establishes the rules of procedure: 'Die he or justice must.' But though man has nothing with which to expiate his treason, there is, nevertheless, a way out:

> Die he or justice must; unless for him
> Some other able, and as willing, pay
> The rigid satisfaction, death for death. (3. 210–12)

That 'other' is to be the Son, who in his love for humankind is indeed willing to be the means of grace (3. 228). Fallen human beings can do nothing to effect their salvation, says the Son. 'Behold me then,' he tells his Father, 'me for him, life for life / I offer, on me let thine anger fall; / Account me Man' (3. 236–8). Thus the graceful purposes of love, we are to understand, operate through a rather chilling, stony-eyed insistence on rigid satisfaction; life for life, death for death.

Milton's is a classic expression of the so-called penal substitutionary theory of the atonement. Christ is punished instead of human beings. A contemporary statement of this theory is to be found in the Doctrinal Basis of the Universities and Colleges Christian Fellowship (UCCF) which holds as a fundamental truth of Christianity, 'Redemption from the guilt, penalty and power of sin only through the sacrificial death once and for all time of our representative and substitute, Jesus Christ.'[4] One of the problems that has been felt with this theory is that, though it seeks to save the justice of God, it fails to do precisely that – for how can it be just for an innocent person to suffer the penalty for another's guilt? Questions of injustice aside, however, that God's anger has to be worked out is a grim thought. And, even if we suspend consideration of God's anger, a grim sense of an unpleasant obligation that has to be gone through with remains: 'the rigid satisfaction, death for death'.

Substitutionary theories of the atonement are particular versions of what can be grouped together as satisfaction theories, and the great strength of satisfaction theories is the strong appeal they make to our desire that things should be put right. This is not just a desire that all should turn out happily in our being saved, but that there should be a restoration of order and equilibrium; it is a desire that things should be put back into balance in such a way that complete moral equity obtains in their final order. There is a moral purity and tidiness about satisfaction theories of how the atonement works and that is in a way pleasing: God's demand for – and our desire for – cosmic justice are well met, but it is a stern business.

At Langland's Hell's gate the light is demanding entry and within Hell panic is mounting. The devils, most of them, know the game is up. Satan recognises the light as just like the one that came and took Lazarus. Lucifer,[5] however, stands on his rights:

> If he deprives me of my right, he'll be robbing me by force,
> For by right and good reason, the people who are here
> Are mine body and soul, both the good and the evil.
> For he himself said, who is Lord of heaven,
> That if Adam ate the apple everyone should die
> And dwell in pain with us devils – that's the threat he made.
>
> (276–80)

This doesn't carry much conviction with the other devils. Lucifer got possession of the human race through guile in an act of treason against his Lord – so the devils have no genuine entitlement to them. Satan says to Lucifer:

> You got them with guile and broke into his garden
> And looking like a snake sat in the apple tree
> And urged her to eat, Eve on her own,
> And told her a story full of treasonous words.
> And in this way you got them out and brought them finally here.
> But if guile's at the bottom, the thing's not duly obtained.
>
> (286–91)

And Goblin says:

> God will not be beguiled or fooled.
> We have no true title to them,
> because treason got them condemned. (292–3)

The devils' confabulation is interrupted by the light speaking again to demand entrance:

> Dukes of this dim place, undo these gates at once,
> That Christ may come in, the King of heaven's son. (320–21)

And at these words Hell breaks open. And now those who dwell in darkness have seen a great light; the mighty God will set them free. It is accomplished. Nevertheless, before leading souls out of Hell Christ takes care to meet Lucifer's claim about his rights. In fact, he takes surprising care given that the devils themselves have already denied the entitlement. The first thing he does after breaking into Hell is offer his soul to Lucifer in *amendes*, in satisfaction. It seems that there is after all a measure of legitimacy in Lucifer's claim and that Christ wants to be seen to act justly. Anyway, due restitution is going to be made. The language of Langland's Christ reminds one of Milton:

> All that man has misdone, I, man, will amend it.
> Member for member was amends by the Old Law,
> And life for life also – and by that law I claim
> Adam and all his issue at my will hereafter. (342–5)

And so all is above board – the demands of justice are satisfied:

> So don't suppose, Lucifer, I fetch them against the law
> But by right and good reason here I ransom my liegemen.
>
> (349–50)

Thus our desire that due and equitable redress should be made is met. Member for member, life for life, death for death: pleasing parities, proper balance; equilibrium restored. And yet there are questions as to how much the principle of justice is being honoured. Christ offers amends, a ransom, satisfaction – and yet isn't there a deceitfulness about that offer, for there is no question of Lucifer really being given Christ's soul to keep? It's hardly fair exchange, soul for soul. Again,

when Christ asserts that his dealings with humankind involve the operation of 'mercy through righteousness' (390), there is something slip-
pery about the way in which he seeks to prove his point:

> It is not the custom on earth to hang a criminal
> More than once, even if he's a traitor.
> And if the king of a kingdom should come at that time
> When a criminal's to suffer death or punishment,
> Law desires that he grant him life, if he looks on him.
> And I who am King of Kings shall come at that time
> When judgement condemns to death all who are wicked.
> And if law wants me to look on them, it's down to my grace
> Whether they die or don't die for the evil they've done.
>
> (380–88)

There's a shifting from one justification for the exercise of clemency to
another here – first the notion that you can't punish someone for the
same crime twice, then the appearance of the king and the requirement
that the criminal be spared, then Christ's claim that, required by law 'to
look on' the criminals, he can as supreme king exercise grace, if he so
wishes. And that slipperiness may indicate a feeling on Langland's part
that none of these justifications really does – none of them convinc-
ingly makes the case for justice because the condemned person gets off
through a legal technicality or the exercise of arbitrary power. If *law* is
served, *justice* isn't. It isn't clear whether Langland or his Christ really
think the argumentation is telling. There is a suggestion that Christ's
tongue is in his cheek as he offers his tricksy justifications to Lucifer. Is
he perhaps just teasing when he makes claims for the justice of his
mercy? Possibly – but clearly, the bottom line *is* mercy – for
humankind, anyway:

> Fiends and fiendlings before me shall stand
> And be at my bidding to go wherever I please,
> But to be merciful to mankind, my nature requires it,
> For we are brethren by blood. (374–7)

Christ's being a man *requires* that he be merciful to mankind. You could
see this natural obligation to mercy as a kind of justice, mercy being
what *ought* to be offered, but equally you could see it as something that

obstructs strict justice. Certainly it's one law for fiends and another for human beings:

> my righteousness and right shall rule all hell
> And mercy all mankind before me in heaven. (397–8)

Hell gets righteousness, 'all mankind before me in heaven' get mercy. How equitable is that? And the contrast between mercy and righteousness here itself suggests that when it comes to his kin Christ ignores considerations of justice in favour of mercy; indeed, the suggestion that he would be an 'unkynde' king unless he helped his relatives (399; 'unkynde' here means 'unnatural', and suggests 'unfamilial' as well as meaning 'unkind' in the modern sense) may contain an irony on the nepotism natural to earthly rulers – but apparently all right in the God Man.

As we have seen, on first breaking into Hell, Christ appeals to certain parities to meet Lucifer's cries of foul and prove the legitimacy of what he is doing. However, the claims that justice is being served are not always unequivocally supported by the appeal to parity. When Christ invokes 'an eye for an eye and a tooth for a tooth', he uses it not just in reference to the exchange of himself for humankind, but in reference to a matching of modes of action – the ways in which he and the devil operate are in a sense one:

> With guile you got them, against what was right.
> For in my palace of Paradise in the form of a snake
> You fetched there falsely that which I loved.
> Thus like a reptile with a lady's face
> Thievishly you robbed me; the Old Law permits
> Beguilers to be beguiled – and that's a good method:
> A tooth for a tooth and an eye for an eye.[6]
> And so soul shall pay for soul, and sin cover sin,
> And all that man has misdone, I, man, will amend it. (335–42)

So is God a beguiler, a deceiver, a trickster? That's how Mercy (in line with some patristic thinking) sees it:

> And just as through a beguiler's guile man was beguiled
> So shall grace that all began make a good end
> And beguile the beguiler. (159–61)

Christ himself confirms this notion that grace is a beguilement of the powers of evil:

> You fetched what was mine in my place against all notions of
>   right –
> Falsely and felonously; good faith taught me
> To recover them by ransom, and by no other method,
> So that what you gained with guile is won back through grace.
> You, Lucifer, in the likeness of a snake
> Got by guile those whom God loved;
> And I in the likeness of a mortal man – who am Lord of heaven –
> Have graciously requited your guile – let guile meet guile!
> And as Adam and all the rest died by means of a tree,
> Adam and all the rest shall come to life by means of a tree;
> And guile is beguiled and fallen into his guile . . .
> Now your guile begins to turn back on you
> And my grace to grow ever greater and wider. (351–63)

What the incarnation and crucifixion accomplish is an aesthetically delightful matching of action to action, precise tit-for-tat which enhances the pleasure of the villain getting his come-uppance. The pleasure of these patterns is joined by the satisfactions of irony as Lucifer falls into the pit he has dug, is hoist in his own petard; his guile turns out to be self-destructive; it seems it will disappear centripetally up its own backside into nothing, while the grace of God is a massive centrifugal force which will spread through the whole Universe.

Grace turns the threateningness of the Old Law, its grimness, into something in which we can rejoice. The Old Law's eye for an eye is about rigid satisfaction, but in Langland's vision grace converts the Old Law into a means by which God pays back the devil in two senses. He discharges a debt, but he also gives as good as he has got in a way that parodies the idea of true equity – you cheat me, I'll cheat you back. In 'good faith' Gods pays the ransom, and he also keeps faith with this Father of falsehood and his lies precisely by deceiving him.

This feels far from grim; there's great delight to be taken in all this as the boot is put onto the other foot and firmly in on the devil. There is also available the subversive pleasure of watching clever deception flourish – enjoyment, too, in the subversive notion that the God of justice and righteousness is the author of this deception. And so the atonement comes to feel comic, comic not just in the sense of having a happy ending, but in the sense of being something to laugh about. Amidst the laughter, however, amidst the comic anarchy of one bad turn deserving and getting another, what price righteousness? For all the satisfying matching up and balancing of this and that, you hardly feel moral equity has been given the lead role.

With Christ's deployment of guile and his not wholly satisfactory arguments to justify his actions, with the implication of a nepotistic favouritism towards humankind, there is a sense in Langland's presentation of what is going on in the atonement that a fast one is being pulled, a loophole being exploited. When the daughters of God first meet, Truth and Righteousness are very confident that the destiny of humankind is Hell. This suggests that if strict justice, which these attributes of God represent, were to rule the day, then humankind would indeed be damned perpetually. As it turns out, however, Truth and Righteousness are quite wrong; and their eventual concession to Peace's perspective (418–22) dramatises the submission of justice to mercy.

As the sisters make things up Peace says: 'Let no people perceive that we quarrelled; / For nothing is impossible to Him that is almighty' (420–21). Langland's probing of the psalm text in which the allegory of the daughters of God is grounded – 'Mercy and Truth have met together, Righteousness and Peace have kissed each other' (Ps. 85:10) – suggests a reason for the embrace, a prior quarrel. The poet's treatment of that quarrel discloses an apparent disequilibrium between God's justice and his mercy with the balance on the side of mercy. Maybe in the unfathomable being of God the principles are in fact reconciled, for with God nothing is impossible;[7] but human understanding – to the point at which it confesses its inability to discern – has to see mercy as primary. In human perspectives, limited and provisional as they are (perhaps Langland ought to have heeded Peace's injunction and not allowed anyone to see the quarrel between the daughters of God), God's love drives the action of the atonement and never mind if justice is slighted.[8]

How, after all, can it be just that we sinners are saved, given that we ourselves can do nothing to put right the wrong we have committed? If I have wronged you, I might seek to balance my offence by a compensating good deed, but if someone else does that deed on my behalf it is not clear that strict justice has been served, even if adequate compensation has been given. Langland's way of putting things acknowledges this and celebrates the injustice of grace, the inequity of love.[9] For love will find a way, even if it has to be a guileful one.

That it is love rather than justice that drives the atonement explains the exuberance of Langland's writing, the comedy, the verve, the enthusiasm, the anarchy. The extravagant, celebratory tone arises out of Langland's perception that the atonement process is something God positively wants rather than one to which, as it were, he finds he has to assent. In Milton there is a component of regret in God's attitude to the atonement. Though the Father loves his human creation, saving it is something of an inconvenience. The Father tell the Son:

> well thou know'st how dear
> To me are all my works, nor man the least,
> Though last created, that for him I spare
> Thee from my bosom and right hand, to save,
> By losing thee awhile, the whole race lost. (3. 276–80)

It's a shame that the Son should have to leave the Father. And then what is primary in the motivation of the Son is not first and foremost love of man, but filial obedience:

> his meek aspect
> Silent yet spake, and breathed immortal love
> To mortal men, above which only shone
> Filial obedience: as a sacrifice
> Glad to be offered, he attends the will
> Of his great Father. (3. 266–71)

In this elevation of obedience primacy is accorded to the doing of duty, to the fulfilling of obligation. More abstractly, what is apparent is the determining role of antecedent states of affairs, of the past. The Son performs the atonement in accordance with a prior stipulation of the Father. In Milton, and in satisfaction theories generally, the atonement is a response; it is something that has to happen because something else has happened first. What it accomplishes is a goal set by what has happened in the past. In Langland's vision God's love is not made to flow down channels moulded by the past. This is why God's original promulgation of man's doom is treated so cavalierly; it's why pressure is put on our normal, antecedent understandings of God. The process of atonement comes to be seen as a positive opportunity for God, not a way in which he meets his own demands. The atonement is profoundly creative rather than restorative. For instance, it opens the way to the full satisfaction of a desire within God.

> For I who am lord of life, love is my drink,
> And on account of that drink today I died upon earth.
> I fought so hard for man's sake I am still thirsty.[10]
> No drink can refresh me or slake my thirst
> Until the vintage falls in the valley of Jehosaphat
> And I can drink the first new wine of the resurrection of the
> dead. (366–71)

And then, by acheiving the final well-being of humanity the atonement makes the suffering and death occasioned by sin ultimately good:

> If people didn't know suffering, they'd never know happiness;
> For no one who hasn't suffered knows what happiness is . . .
> A really rich man living in comfort and ease
> Wouldn't know what suffering was, unless in nature's course
> there was death. (204–5, 209–10)

So God permits man to sin and thereby allows him to appreciate the joys of heaven which the atonement secures. It is not that the unpleasantness of things following the Fall is simply made of no account, but that that unpleasantness plays its role in the establishment of a positive state of affairs. We can discern this process in the way the atonement produces an enlargement of God's experience and knowledge through an exposure to the negatives of human experience. Perhaps, in fact, the considerations in the passage just quoted apply even to God's own knowledge. That passage continues:

> So God, who began everything out of his good will,
> Became man of a maiden to save mankind
> And experienced being sold to see the sorrow of dying . . .
> For till we encounter having little, I may well say,

No one, as I suppose, knows what 'enough' means.
And so God, in his goodness, the first man, Adam –
He established him in happiness and the greatest joy,
And then he let him sin, so as to feel sorrow –
To know what happiness was – really to know it.
And after that God ventured himself and took Adam's nature
To know what he (God? Adam?) has suffered / experienced
    in three different places
In heaven and on earth – and now he's going to hell
To know what absolute suffering is,
    he who knows what is absolute joy. (211–13, 215–24)

The atonement, then, can be seen to accomplish not so much the restoration of a right order which has been damaged, as the evolution of a new and better order in fulfilment of the creative purposes of love. On this view the Fall is truly a *felix culpa*, a fortunate event, which permits an exuberant creativity to flourish to the full, for instance, by transforming negatives into positives; what is accomplished is the fullest outworking of the purposes of love, which could not have occurred without the Fall. On this view the Fall and what flows from it in incarnation and crucifixion liberates rather than constrains the creative love of God; indeed it liberates God to become something better than he has been. What is accomplished can be seen as the fulfilment of a far richer and fuller plan than that of righting the wrong of the Fall in a satisfying of the demands of justice.[11]

These perspectives allow us to understand the elision of suffering in John's 'passion' narrative and to appreciate why that narrative ends not in a cry of dereliction, but in a shout of triumph: 'It is accomplished!' What happens at the crucifixion is so good, so perfectly expressive of God's love, so creative of the new and better that regret for what crucifixion involves by way of physical pain and mental suffering gets pushed out of the picture. It is a triumph – the crucifixion at the bottom line is not about abasement and suffering, but about achievement and victory. This victory does not merely recoup enemy gains – it uses those apparent gains as the means of enhancing and extending its own achievements. What is accomplished is not so much a simple defeat of evil as a using of evil for creative purposes; evil is made the agent of a divine purpose which is the fullest possible unfolding of love and grace and goodness through the created universe and within the very being of God.

Satisfaction theories of the atonement, centred as they are on the achievement of justice, have God looking to the state in which he exists in self-sufficiency as a standard by which all is to be judged, to his holiness, to his righteousness and to a state of the universe in which sin did not exist. It is a backward-looking perspective, limiting, reductive, and perhaps also self-centred. It may be preferable to see and feel the atonement as the means of realisation of our perfect God's forward-looking, creative, permissive, and entirely unegocentric impulse not to rest in his holiness but always to move out to the flawed Other in love, to accept it and redeem it. The realisation of this impulse, though it might even seem to compromise God's perfect justice, turns out to bring with it the fulfilment of God himself. The completion of a God joyously bound to his creature as the God of perfect love – that is the ultimate accomplishment of the process of atonement.

IN THE DARK YOU SEE A LIGHT. A CROSS, blazing with light, quarters the night sky. The cross is richly decorated with gold, and you notice in particular five fine jewels. It is beautiful, but terrifying, for it makes you conscious of your moral ugliness, your sin. You look away, but your eyes are drawn back; and now it is not jewels and gold you see, but blood. You see no body, but the cross is streaming with blood. You are horrified; but now you cannot look away, and as you gaze, so the gold and the jewels and the beauty return and the blood disappears – and then again you see blood instead of the gold. This oscillation of blood and gold, beauty and horror, is continuous. As it goes on, you begin to hear the cross speak.

It tells you a story of violence and suffering; how it was cut down at a forest's edge and made to serve as a gallows; it tells you how it was pierced with nails; it tells you how it was made to kill the one whom it acknowledged as its Lord. It tells you how it wanted to fall down upon its Lord's enemies and destroy them, and how it dared not because its Lord wished otherwise. It tells you how, after the execution, it was cut down and buried in a pit. It is a grim tale.

It is not finished, however. The cross tells you how it was found by its Lord's disciples, taken from its place of burial and given its rich decoration. It tells you how it is now venerated as a tree of victory, how now, no longer abject and broken, it towers above creation, honoured as the means of salvation, a thing of glory.

The picture changes. You see Christ getting ready for battle; young, brave, vigorous. He strips himself, a warrior who needs no weapons; he is eager to ascend the cross, the place of conflict. He wants this thing to happen, for he wants to redeem humankind. That is what he came to do, and this is the consummation. Now he is on the cross. You know he must suffer, but you don't see it at first, you see only serenity, joy even. This battle is going to be won.

But then you look again and you see the blood, you see the wide wounds around the nails, you see the flesh scraped and pierced by the crown of thorns; you see Christ's body shrivel and wizen; you see the pallor of death on his face; you wait for the moment of his passing; you wait and wait, your sorrow at his sorrow growing; you want an end to what he is having to endure. You want him to die and the horror to be over. But just when you think he is going to die, instead you see him, there on the cross, smile. For this is what he wants; it is not to him a grim necessity – he would suffer more if he could, even though that greater suffering were not necessary to save us. His love is extravagant, unmeasured, and so his suffering is a joy, a bliss, an endless delight to him. It accomplishes his victory over evil and our salvation, and it achieves for him his fulfilment.*

* After *The Dream of the Rood* and Julian of Norwich.

8

'Father, into thy hands I commit my spirit!'
(Luke 23:46)

HELEN CUNLIFFE

'Having said this, he breathed his last.'

At the very end, Jesus speaks words of the deepest trust. He has struggled to understand the truth about himself, has spent a lifetime working it out, testing it out, receiving pieces of the jigsaw puzzle from the acts he was able to perform, from his prayer and times with God, from the insights of friends and foes. At the very end of his life he realises that all that has happened has led to this point. All he has ever been, or signified to others, has brought him to this; to this moment of recognition, this moment of truth.

At the same time he also knows now that all that has happened – and however the story may continue to unfold – is not essential to him now. Only the deepest truth now matters; and only the love of Father for Son, and of Son for Father, exists. And so leaning against God, who is all that's left and all there has ever been, Jesus breathes his last. There is no further agony to endure, nothing can hurt more than it does now, and nothing can hurt again. All is finished, it is accomplished. He can let go. He sighs away his soul into the Father's keeping, and breathes his last.

This is our story too. We live alone, we die alone. But there, as a dim memory from our beginning, recollected whenever there is bliss in this world, and sometimes strangely at the heart of tragedy, is the love of the Father for us. There, at the end, when all the wondering and all the questioning is over, if we will let go, we too will find that God's love waits to receive us.

God's love working in us leads us to try in our turn to demonstrate to our poor, torn world the way back to that love that made us; to that love that would sustain us, as it supported our Lord, if only, like him, we would let go and lean into it.

'Father, into thy hands I commit my spirit!' These words of deep trust, spoken by Christ at the moment of the absolute end, represent the taking of the truth of this moment into himself. And so for us as well. We live alone, we die alone; the frustration of our lives in this world – all our broken relationships, our betrayals, our murders – are because we know we shall never be understood by one another. It is our grief, the 'human tragedy' that, knowing this, we still so badly want to be understood and accepted. The classic faith statement is that it is only in God that we shall find the intimate relationship we long for, the absolute mutuality we crave. More recently theologians have suggested that this is why we 'construct' God: that it is precisely because we know it is beyond our own capabilities to solve this dislocation deep within us that we seek an all-knowing, all-powerful being with whom we can relate.

Christian thinkers throughout the centuries have struggled to find ways to describe this state of isolation and alienation, this sense of being 'away from home', ill at ease in the world. 'Our hearts are restless until they find their rest in you,' wrote St Augustine in the second century.[1] Also recognising this truth, St Columba in the sixth century spoke of finding solace for his sense of isolation in God alone:

> Alone with none but thee, my God,
> I journey on my way.
> What shall I fear if thou art near,
> O King of night and day?
> More safe am I within thy hand
> Than if a host did round me stand.[2]

John of the Cross's poetry, written in the sixteenth century, faces us with this same sense of restlessness in the world. He describes a desire to be with God so deep that death would be a mercy, for life is hollow:

> I live without inhabiting
> Myself – in such a wise that I
> Am dying that I do not die.
>
> Within myself I do not dwell
> Since without God I cannot live.
> Reft of myself, and God as well,
> What serves this life (I cannot tell)
> Except a thousand deaths to give?
> Since waiting here for life I lie
> And die because I do not die.[3]

This awareness is echoed by the twentieth-century poet T. S. Eliot who, for instance, in 'Ash Wednesday', referred to the 'torment of love unsatisfied, the greater torment of love satisfied',[4] a cry echoed by saints and mystics in every age.

Two distinctive ecclesiologies – ways in which the Church has understood itself – have marked the development of the English Church. The influence of the great sixth-century reformer of monasticism, St Benedict, found expression through the work of his disciple St Wilfred, who sought to establish Roman traditions firmly in these islands. St Benedict, in his Rule, had stressed a stability of lifestyle based upon the material security of well-built and endowed monasteries.[5] St Wilfred, following St Benedict, saw the success of a community as partly dependent upon its increasing ownership of land, and defined stability, as opposed to *peregrinatio* (wandering) as a virtue. Contrast this attitude with that of followers of the Celtic tradition in the same early English Church, who had no money and owned very little land to build on. Their love of the natural order and their appreciation of nature in all its moods suggests that even without the constraints of limited resources they would have developed what Adrian Hastings describes as a 'preoccupation with asceticism and an enthusiastic dependence' upon God's providence.[6]

Interestingly, Hastings points out the importance of roads to the Roman tradition, both for the ease of journeying, cutting down the time of travel, and therefore facilitating effective pastoral care. For the Celts, on the other hand, the journey was almost the whole point of the exercise, and inaccessibility – what was termed the 'white martydom' – was to them very desirable. Many recent spiritual writers have suggested the importance of the rediscovery of our Celtic roots, as far as we can: and *peregrinatio* attracts increasing numbers, at least for as long as their leave entitlement allows!

A recent experience of following St Cuthbert's Way, from Melrose to Lindisfarne, in company with other pilgrims, has persuaded me of the spiritual benefits of walking prayerfully. Undertaking that journey represented for us a new way of encountering God, which some of us may not find easy in settled places, even churches. It's important to know that, if religious buildings and organised religion don't draw you closer to God, that doesn't mean that there's nowhere else to look. Engaging literally with solitude and silence, in the company of others about the same endeavour, and doing so in the context of an actual journey, is for some of us somehow to 'go with the grain'. Perhaps for more of us than we realise – for those, perhaps, who seek solace for our painful human loneliness through the pursuit of constant company which, we discover, only makes matters worse. Going home alone after the party is something we hate to do, and try not to have to do – and the messes we get ourselves into in order to avoid doing so are, as the man said, legion.

A discovery of pilgrimage has worked for me; it offers a necessary balance to the formal worship in which I am so often engaged. Other people will find other ways of facing up to and coming to terms with the realities of self and life in the world; other places in which to learn to recognise and accept the permanent ache we live with as a normal human response to separation from God. But then, into every life come times of acute distress and intense suffering. How do Jesus' words of trust sound against such demands as these? As we reflect on the cross, we realise that Jesus had prepared, consciously or not, for this moment of final surrender all his life. If we are wise, so will we. Not by seeking out opportunities to endure suffering – that would be pathological, and mad – but by recognising the 'small deaths' that come our way in the course of life, and by naming them and growing spiritually through them.

First, perhaps we can learn to recognise such moments of testing, as the first desperate pain of separation begins to subside, as places of growth, and by doing so come to know that there are times in our life when we simply cannot do anything but let go, and lean upon what we have built so far – lean upon what God in the kindness of his provision for us, in the world that surrounds us, has placed there for our sustaining. This leads, secondly, to the cultivation of stewardship. Stewardship is often understood as a task of management in relation to God's gifts to us through the created order, and therefore often as a rather practical, domestic, or even church-organisational affair. However, there is a further, more profound, dimension to stewardship, which is also to do with letting go. Stewardship is concerned to teach us to acknowledge that none of this is ours, and that all is God's: that 'we brought nothing into the world, so that we can take nothing out of it' (1 Tim. 6:7). Initially disconcerting, this attitude to life is ultimately liberating, and leads us further along the path that will one day enable us to pray with Christ and with confidence, 'Father, into thy hands I commit my spirit!'

As with individuals, so with communities. These are strange days for the Church, as we try to balance news of an apparent increase in attendance with an awareness of a decrease in membership; and of an unprecedented interest in spirituality, with a decrease in baptisms, church weddings, and church funerals. We have lived for many years upon our memories of days long gone; it is now time we woke up and looked about us.

These days offer us a golden opportunity to consider afresh what's essential to the Church's message, and what has become, over the passage of time, irrelevant 'clutter'. As when clearing granny's attic, it is tempting to take with you every last thing – baby shoes and first books, graduation photos and back copies of Punch – and in some circumstances that's both possible and justifiable. They don't make those sorts of shoes any more, so it's interesting to keep them. But perhaps the place for them is a museum. And of course it depends what you're taking the items in question for. Are you going to use them? Or might they just 'come in handy'? (They won't!) If you're moving to another big old house with an attic, there's probably no harm in taking quite a lot of things with you. But if, for example, you were packing for a journey upon which you could only take those things you could carry, then quite a lot will have to be left behind. Christians are constantly challenged to understand themselves to be on a journey: 'For here we have no lasting city' (Heb. 13:14). In what sense then can the Church today be said to be ready, packed, and prepared to move on at a moment's notice?

The Gospel is always challenged to be responsive to the culture that surrounds it. A faith centred on an incarnate God is a pretty big hint that any attempt to distinguish between Church and the world as the arena of God's love and promise is wrong-headed. In his day, Jesus urged others to notice and respond to the signs of the times, and we should do the same. The ability to recognise what's going on around us brings with it the maturity to handle the situation. We are never tested beyond our powers.

For example, in our day and in our society we see the challenges confronting education, health provision, and law and order. We also know that two things in particular would help greatly to meet these challenges: more money, given both by willing investors and tax-payers, and more people committed to making a difference: more teachers, nurses and doctors. The signs of the times are drawn large, it seems to me, and we can read them. All that stops us responding in a loving way is all that ever has, namely our own selfishness and greed, and our unwillingness to be the first to be generous in case nobody follows. That is a very real risk: nobody followed Christ to the cross, but that didn't make him wrong in his response to his calling.

While countless individual Christians bravely do relate their faith values to our civic life, the Church as a whole seems shy of such an expression of our faith just now. This has not always been the case; the Church has a proud history in the provision of education, medical care and the alleviation of poverty. Of course, in this society the develop-ment of the Welfare State shifted the burden of care to society at large. Today, as society strains to respond to that need, perhaps the churches need to get involved again. As we see the decline of great institutions, such as the National Health Service, we must accept that if we still believed in such institutions we could restore them. Perhaps the Church has some truths to tell here. For example, if the chief reason for an unwillingness to restore public welfare services lies in an unspoken belief that they are being abused, then that belief should be spoken and addressed. If this 'abuse' takes the form of needless over-reliance upon medical practitioners, for example, we might ask whether there is a spiritual root to the nature of this problem of increasing emotional dependency upon others, and set about trying to address it.

There has always been a social dimension to our call to be followers of Christ, and it is to be expected that in each generation this call must be redefined. Perhaps in our generation and society the challenge is to be wise in dealing with those who are not taking the responsibility for their own lives, for whatever reason. C. F. Andrews once defined charity as being 'the accurate response to an actual need'.[7] I would suggest that charity in our time requires addressing the sense of inadequacy and uncertainty that afflicts so many people, which is so closely related to an inability to cope with the complexities of modern living. It is surely here that the Church has something to offer, at once demanding of God's people an heroic engagement with life, while at the same time providing a secure 'home' from which to set out. Helping God's people to discover a God in whom one can place one's trust – and helping them, through accurate support in their actual situations, to understand that they already have all they need for the journey.

This raises questions as to how well the Church understands the contexts in which it is set, and how willing it is to change its ways to embrace them. The cultures that have formed the Church in other parts of the world continue to challenge Western European Christians. Slowly within my own denomination, the Church of England, we are learning to be less prescriptive in our requirements of 'foreign' Anglicans, before we recognise them as 'properly' Anglican. Where I live and work, in the Diocese of Southwark, South London, we are perhaps particularly well placed really to let our guard down, and to explore more fully what Christians brought up in different parts of the Anglican Communion have to offer – more, that is, than simply teaching us how to sing 'Tuma Mina' at the occasional, specially designed, service. As a Church, we have not yet fully grasped what underlies the comment that 'God was in Africa before David Livingstone': God is wherever we go, long before we thought of going there.

Some of the most interesting conversations I've had recently have been to do with the expectations that African Christians now resident in London bring to their churches. I've been aware that when I enter such conversations I'm doing so with very little knowledge and no experience. It's new ground for me, I don't know where it will lead, and it's tempting to retreat into areas – culturally and theologically – where I'm more comfortable. It's tempting to stop listening. Tempting but not good. Not to listen, not to welcome these ways of thinking and these insights into the life of faith, is not only arrogant but is to refuse to trust God. If we don't listen, we might find ourselves looking back in forty years' time and understanding that we failed them, in the same way as we failed those West Indian Christians who came here forty years ago and now worship separately in almost exclusively black churches.

This particularly interesting challenge to us, in our quest of learning to trust God, and letting go of controlling God, has been explored by the missionary priest Vincent Donovan. His pioneering and prophetic work with the Masai has not received the attention it deserves.[8] Donovan set out intending to take Christianity to the Masai in East Africa. Instead, he learned to listen and to hear from the tribespeople what God had already done and was in the process of doing in their lives. Through the telling of stories and through the sharing of hopes, Donovan came to see that God was indeed already at work, and so his task came to be to draw parallels between the stories he heard from their tradition and the stories he brought from his.

All of which leads naturally into a third concern for the Church at the start of the twenty-first century: namely, how we should relate to peoples of other faiths. This is an imperative that we've regarded until now as something of an option, perhaps as a slightly crazy speciality. But while many of us have chosen to ignore the implications of the growth of the 'global village', none of us could ignore the events of 11 September 2001. The choice is now starkly before us: we can either retreat, and pretend that nothing has happened – and if threatened, respond with the politics of a Le Pen; or we can go forward in trust, and seek earnestly to find places to meet, points of contact.

When I asked one of our Cathedral choristers recently what he thought a church was for, he said, 'It should be generous. It should look after the poor, and provide a place to worship.' Compare this with the first three of the five Pillars of Islam: the first, that you should declare the testimony of faith, witnessing and sharing your belief that there is only one God; the second, that you should perform your five daily prayers; the third, that you should pay your poor-due of at least 2.5 per cent of your annual income. These two understandings of God's love abroad in the world are not so far removed, and surely provide common – and crucial – ground to work on.

As I prepared this chapter, the children in our communities in SE1 were puzzled and frightened following the events of 11 September. They noted the increased presence of police upon the streets near their homes and schools, and it did nothing to reassure them. They looked up when planes went over, and some were reduced to tears by a new sort of bullying: younger children teased by older ones who pointed to a plane in the sky, saying that it was getting bigger, coming closer . . . We also had some horrible, racist, anti-Islamic literature left around our churches by political activists. Both examples remind us how the raw material for war is always present in human hearts, waiting and ready to be called upon.

How might we, as members of the Christian Church, respond to these fault-lines that divide human beings? Again, 'letting go' is the key. Would an appropriate reaction to 11 September – for the sake of the whole world and all the people of faith in it – be for one of the world faiths to 'go first', and dare to invite others to pray alongside them? Not just the leadership – we are used to symbolic acts of unity by faith leaders. Instead, this is a task for local churches, synagogues, mosques and other communities of faith, not least in places where children of different faiths go to school together. Perhaps every Anglican church on a particular day, or every mosque or every synagogue, should open its doors to members of other faiths and say, in effect, 'Into thy hands I commit my spirit!' There is a real challenge here, as making this possible might require us to leave behind some of those beliefs that we hold so dear: for God's sake, as it were, taking leave of God – following, as we do so, the example of our Lord himself, and his first brave disciples.[9]

We do not need to look as far as our relations with other world faiths to see an external mirroring of our internal dislocation. Our Church culture is in danger of alienating us from society at large. No longer can we assume that we live in a 'Christian' society in which the Church is a respected institution whose purpose and language is widely understood. We may not like it, but for the Church's mission to flourish requires a shift in thinking. It is not going to be universally popular to suggest that the role of the churches should be to pursue an heroic quest rather than provide a place of refuge from the pressures of a rapidly changing society. But that is the challenge we face, and just as a missionary to the Masai learnt, we in the churches must not forget that those 'out there' are already God's people, in what is already God's world, that we are set here to serve. In order to do that, what do we need? Maybe a financial or personnel crisis in the Church will help us to focus our thoughts, prayers and efforts in a way that nothing else will. And maybe we should try to make of these days of increased international tension an opportunity to sort out our priorities, and phrase the question posed earlier in this chapter the other way round: not, what do we have to leave behind, but rather, what can we not do without?

'Father, into thy hands I commit my spirit!' It seems then that an interpretation of Christ's words for our days might involve an exercise in greater maturity. The maturity of taking upon ourselves responsibility for our lives, our societies, our planet. A rediscovery of 'charity' follows: an accurate assessment of how things are for us in these days, using the best skills of those people who know how to find out facts, in every area, followed by a generous response where it is needed, in whatever form is needed. And this, though working of course for the good of our society, our world, brings spiritual benefits. For, at the end, perhaps we shall be able to stand where Christ stood, during his life, able to choose well the way ahead at every crossroad, able to see clearly into every issue. Standing where Christ stood equals standing alone and fully present. No excuses, no blame – 'it is as it is'.

Christ's words of deep trust from the cross, his full presence to himself in his need, and to his God, carry no blame, no threat – they carry nothing but love. Love lived out in the service of those around him, and love lived out in the one soul he was absolutely and utterly responsible for – his own. Perhaps, having tried to live such a life, we shall at the end be able to say as he did, 'Father, into thy hands I commit my spirit!', and know ourselves to be greeted by those incredible words, that Christ said would greet such a one: 'Well done, good and faithful servant.'

THE COURTESY OF GOD, WHO, AS Thomas Traherne put it, 'courts our love with infinite esteem', is something that we would do well to re-emphasise in our days. Interviewed for our cathedral newsletter, a 90-year-old member of our congregation said that she regretted the anger she sees around her in the world; in our days there seems to be more of an emphasis upon rights than responsibilities. And while it is the case that some ground needed to be reclaimed for those who have few rights, perhaps we have gone far enough for now in that direction. The churches might help society to move through these present tense days into a more level place, by reconsidering this very distinctive strand – the courtesy of God – which is to be found within English mysticism, which I believe depends in its turn upon the respect for the natural order which has come to us from our Celtic roots.

Consider these words of Mother Julian of Norwich; see her love and intimacy with our Lord, and see his with her. Recognise the mutual respect of creature for creator, of creator for creature. Hear the simple pride and pleasure that each feels in the other's presence.

Place yourself in a quiet setting, relax, close your eyes, and picture the cross before you, and our Lord in his suffering upon it. Picture weighing upon him all the troubles and tensions of this world. Call into your mind the burdens you carry, your fears and troubles; speak of them to the Lord. Spend as long as you need unburdening yourself to the Lord. Hear him offer to take your burdens from you. Hear him tell you that he has always carried your burdens for you and will always do so. Hear him speak to you, as he spoke to Julian, and know that in the midst of his personal agony, his awareness of the scale of the world's suffering, he still has time for you . . .

> Then our good Lord Jesus said, 'Are you well satisfied with my suffering for you?' 'Yes, thank you, good Lord,' I replied. 'Yes, good Lord, bless you.' And the kind Lord Jesus said, 'If you are satisfied, I am satisfied too. It gives me great happiness and joy and, indeed, eternal delight ever to have suffered for you. If I could possibly have suffered more, I would have done so.'[10]

Remain in quiet thankfulness, and, if you think you can, commit yourself afresh to God's service, with Julian's own words, 'Yes, thank you, good Lord . . . Yes, good Lord, bless you.'

Introduction (Richard Harries)

1. John Wilkinson, *Egeria's Travels* (Warminster, Aris & Phillips, 1999), pp. 75–7, 154–7.
2. Herbert Thurston, *Lent and Holy Week* (London, 1906), pp. 383–4.
3. Ibid., p. 386.
4. Alonso Messia (trans. with an introduction by Herbert Thurston), *The Devotion of the Three Hours' Agony on Good Friday* (London, Sands and Co., 1899), p. 4.
5. From a broadcast on BBC Radio 4, 31 July 1981.

1: The cross in the 21st century (Rowan Williams)

1. Charles Causley, *Collected Poems 1951–1975* (London, Macmillan, 1975), p. 69.

2: 'Father, forgive them; for they know not what they do' (Edmund Newell)

1. Friedrich Heer, *God's First Love: Christians and Jews over Two Thousand Years* (London, Weidenfeld & Nicolson, 1999), pp. 36–7.
2. St Chrysostom, *Sixth Oration Against the Jews*.
3. Quoted in Heer, p. 37.
4. Quoted in Gareth Lloyd Jones, *Hard Sayings: Difficult New Testament Texts for Jewish–Christian Dialogue* (London, Council of Christians and Jews, 1993), p. 16.
5. St Eusebius, *Demonstrations of the Gospel*, 1.7.
6. Quoted in Robert S. Wistrich, *Antisemitism: The Longest Hatred* (London, Methuen, 1991), p. 13.
7. Quoted in Eugene J. Fisher, 'Passion Plays from a Christian Point of View', *Anti Semitism in Passion Plays* (www.passionplayusa.org/dialog.htm).
8. Quoted in Lloyd Jones, p. 5.
9. Quoted in Wistrich, p. 39.
10. Quoted in Helen P. Fry (ed.), *Christian–Jewish Dialogue: A Reader* (Exeter, 1996), pp. 10–11.
11. Quoted in Charlotte Klein, *Anti-Judaism in Christian Theology* (London, SPCK, 1978), p. 118.
12. See Martin Dudley, 'The Jews in the Good Friday Liturgy', *Anglican Theological Review*, 76:1 (1994).
13. James Shapiro, *Oberammergau: The Troubling Story of the World's Most Famous Passion Play* (London, Little, Brown, 2000), p. 28.

3: 'Truly, I say to you, today you will be with me in Paradise' (Giles Fraser)

1. René Girard, *I See Satan Fall Like Lightning*, (Leominster, Gracewing, 2001), p. 37.
2. Tom Wolfe, 'Pornoviolence', in *Mauve Gloves and Madmen, Clutter and Vine* (New York, Bantam, 1977), pp. 161–2.

3. Bryan Cheyette, review, *Times Literary Supplement*, 18 February 1994.
4. Gillian Rose, *Mourning Becomes the Law: Philosophy and Representation* (Cambridge University Press, 1996), p. 43.
5. Ibid., pp. 45–6.
6. Mary Midgely, *Wickedness: A Philosophical Essay* (London, Routledge, 1984), p. 114.
7. Ibid., p. 115.
8. Christopher Browning, *Ordinary Men: Reserve Police Battalion 101 and the Final Solution in Poland* (New York, HarperCollins, 1992), pp. 56–7.
9. Ibid., pp. 66–7.
10. Ibid., p. 189.
11. W. H. Auden, *For the Time Being* (London, Faber & Faber, 1945), p. 113.
12. Ibid., p. 113.
13. Ibid., p. 117.
14. Rose, *Mourning Becomes the Law*, p. 52.
15. Ibid., p. 54.

4: 'Woman, behold, your son!. . . Behold, your mother!' (Peter Doll)

1. *The English Hymnal*, Appendix, No. 3 (Oxford University Press, 1933).
2. Quoted in Aymer Vallance, *Old Crosses and Lychgates* (London, B. T. Batsford, 1920), p. 6.
3. St John Chrysostom, Homily *On the burial place and the cross*, 2.
4. Ibid.

5: 'Eli, Eli, lama sabachthani?. . . My God, my God, why hast thou forsaken me?' (Tarjei Park)

1. David Scott, *Selected Poems* (Bloodaxe Books, 1998), p. 47.
2. Elie Wiesel, *The Trial of God* (Schocken, 1995), pp. vii, xxiii.
3. 'Loving the Torah more than God' in *Yosl Rakover Talks to God* (Jonathan Cape, 1999), p. 81.
4. Ibid., pp. 23–5.
5. Bob Dylan, 'A Hard Rain's A-Gonna Fall' on *The Freewheelin' Bob Dylan* (CBS, 1963).
6. Ateliers et Presses de Taizé, F-71250 Taizé-Communauté.

6: 'I thirst' (Sabina Alkire)

1. Quoted from the Constitution of the Missionaries of Charity in George Gorraee, *For Love of God: Mother Teresa of Calcutta* (London, T. Shand Alba Publications, 1974).
2. 'Whatever You Did Unto One of the Least, You Did Unto Me', Mother Teresa MC in Michael Collopy, *Works of Love are Works of Peace* (Ignatius Press, 1996), pp. 191–6.
3. Ibid.
4. Mother Teresa's last letter, 5 September 1997 (the day she died). http://www.tisv.be/mt/lalet.htm
5. Dag Hammarskjöld, *Markings* (New York, Alfred A. Knopf, 1965).
6. William Blake, 'The Little Black Boy', originally in *Songs of Innocence and Experience*, quoted in Arthur Quiller-Couch, *The Oxford Book of English Verse: 1250–1900* (Oxford, 1939).
7. Polycarp, *Epistle to the Philippians*, ch. 6, opening sentence.

8. Except perhaps *Sublimus Dei*, 1537, on the enslavement and evangelization of Indians.

9. Food and Agriculture Organisation of the United Nations, *The State of Food Insecurity in the World 2001*, (Rome, 2001). (815 million).

10. WHO, UNICEF, and WSSCC, *Global Water Supply and Sanitation Assessment* 2000 (Geneva, 2000).

11. The World Bank, *World Development Report* 2003 (Washington DC, 2002).

12. *SIPRI Yearbook 2002: Armaments, Disarmament and International Security* (Oxford, Oxford University Press, 2002). World military expenditure is estimated at $839 billion (in current US dollars).

13. CAFOD *Factsheet* distributed in 2001 (web page outdated).

14. Adapted from CAFOD 2001.

15. Adapted from United Nations Development Program, *Human Development Report 2002: Deepening Democracy in a Fragmented World* (New York, Oxford University Press, 2002), p. 202, chart 15.

16. The World Bank, *Poverty Reduction and the World Bank: Progress in Operationalizing the WDR 2000/2001* (Washington DC, 2001).

17. United Nations Development Program, *Human Development Report 2002*.

18. The World Bank, *Poverty Reduction and the World Bank*.

19. Ibid.

20. World Health Organisation, *World Health Report 2001* (Geneva, 2001).

21. US Center for Disease Control, 'Suicide in the United States', *Factsheet* found at http://www.cdc.gov/ncipc/factsheets/suifacts.htm

22. Ron Sider, 'Take the Pledge: A Practical Strategy for Loving the Poor', *Christianity Today*, 7 September 1998, p. 84.

23. Martin Luther King, Jr, 'A Time to Break Silence', address to Clergy and Laity given at Riverside Church New York, 4 April 1967, reprinted in James M. Washington (ed.), *A Testament of Hope: The Essential Writings and Speeches of Martin Luther King, Jr* (San Francisco, HarperCollins, 1991), p. 241.

24. Germain Grisez, Joseph Boyle and John Finnis, 'Practical Principles, Moral Truth and Ultimate Ends', *American Journal of Jurisprudence*, 32 (1987) pp. 99–151. At p. 128: 'In voluntarily acting for human goods and avoiding what is opposed to them, one ought to choose and otherwise will those and only those possibilities whose willing is compatible with a will toward integral human fulfilment'. [Integral human fulfilment is fulfilment of all human beings including oneself through time in all their dimensions of humanity].

25. For discussion on the Poverty Reduction Strategy Papers and process that emerged from this campaign see www.worldbank.org/poverty/strategies/index.htm

26. Collopy, *Works of Love are Works of Peace*.

27. *Canticle*, 29:3. Reprinted in Kieran Kavanaugh ocd, and Otilio Rodriguez ocd (trans.), *The Collected Works of St John of the Cross* (Washington DC, Institute of Carmelite Studies, 1991), p. 588.

28. Statement by Dag Hammarskjöld, UN Secretary-General 1953–1961, written for the dedication of the United Nations Meditation Room.

29. Quoted and discussed to this effect in Iain Matthews, *Impact of God* (London, Hodder & Stoughton, 1995), p. 97. This is from John's *Canticle* (second redaction) 1:12 see 1:4.

7: 'It is finished' (Hugh White)

1. *Piers Plowman* exists in at least three different versions, probably all by the same author. The version cited here is that known as the B version, written, it seems, around 1377–9. The edition used is that of A. V. C. Schmidt, 2nd edition (London, Dent, 1987), from which I have made translations into something like modern English while trying to preserve the feel of Langland's alliterative verse. Rather than employing end rhymes, this verse works by linking strongly stressed syllables by alliteration. The poem is divided into sections called Passus and all quotations in the text are from Passus 18 of the B version. In the preceding paragraph the line quoted is 187. Further line references are given in the text.

2. *Paradise Lost* was first published in 1667. Quotations from the poem are taken from J. Carey and A. Fowler (eds), *The Poems of John Milton* (Harlow, Longmans, 1968).

3. See PL 3. 132–4.

4. See the UCCF leaflet outlining its Doctrinal Basis. For a powerful and influential statement of the penal substitutionary theory see Karl Barth, *Church Dogmatics*, vol. 4, part 1, section 59, 2: 'The Son of God fulfilled the righteous judgement on us human beings by himself taking our place as a human being, and in our place undergoing the judgement under which we had passed.'

5. Langland conceives Satan and Lucifer (and later Goblin) as separate devilish entities.

6. This line, a biblical quotation, is in Latin as in the original. Such lines of Latin quotation are conventionally not included in the line-count of the poem; hence the apparent discrepancy between the number of lines given in this extract and the line reference.

7. I have understood the 'nothing is impossible to God' idea to have reference to an actual compatibility of mercy and justice which lies beyond the conceptual reach of human beings. It might also, or alternatively, relate to the apparent impossibility of salvation for humankind given all the circumstances (human salvation is at issue in the story of the rich young man when Jesus says that 'with God all things are possible', Matt. 19:26). This would support my claim that Langland presents salvation as something which, as far as human insight goes, ought not to happen, it being contrary to human conceptions of justice.

8. Peace's demand that the sisters' quarrel be concealed implies something transgressive in Langland's showing us that quarrel. This perhaps signals his awareness of the provisional and speculative nature of what he presents in this Passus. After all, if nothing is impossible with God, whatever it seems to human beings must be the case, how can humans hope finally to explain God's action?

9. Langland sees purgatory as a place where the punishment of sin that a retributive justice would demand can be enacted (391–3). But this is more a concession to the principle of justice than a positive affirmation of it; and it should be noted that the length of a person's experience of purgatory is determined by *parce* ('spare' [them]), a principle of mercy, that is, rather than by justice. How could justice determine the measure of punishment for sin, given that sin offends in infinite degree the infinite holiness of God?

10. Absence of punctuation here preserves an appropriate ambiguity. There is also ambiguity (which need not be finally resolved one way of the other) as to whether Christ dies because of a love he already has or because he wants to obtain love, or produce

more love. For is the love something proceeding from God or is it what humankind feels (or will come to feel) for him – or both? Is the resurrection of the dead God's supreme act of love or does it evoke as response supreme love from human beings – or both? However we take these ambiguities, God seems to profit from the process of atonement.

11. Some at least of this may sound like off-the-wall speculation from a theologically irresponsible poet who does after all present himself in his own poem as a lunatic outsider. But a desire to see the process of which the crucifixion is part as something which produces the genuinely new, rather than something the primary purpose of which is to redress a wrong and reinstate a past good, is evident in a more canonical figure than Langland, one who is Langland's near contemporary, Julian of Norwich. In her great vision of the Lord and the servant, Julian finds that the incarnate and ascended Christ has in virtue of his experiences in the world exchanged the old threadbare tunic of Adam for a garment superior in beauty to that worn by the Father himself. For Julian it seems that the process which procures atonement procures also the full achievement of God's nature. See Julian's *Revelations of Divine Love*, of which there are several editions and translations, ch. 51 (in the longer version).

8: 'Father, into thy hands I commit my spirit!' (Helen Cunliffe)

1. St Augustine of Hippo, *Confessions*, book 1, ch. 1, in *Nicene and Post-Nicene Fathers* (Edinburgh, T. & T. Clark, 1994).

2. Attributed to St Columba, one of the 'Prayers before Worship', in Pat Robson (ed.), *A Celtic Liturgy* (London, HarperCollins, 2000).

3. 'Coplas about the soul which suffers with impatience to see God' (trans. Roy Campbell), *Poems of St John of the Cross* (Glasgow, Fount, 1981), p. 35.

4. T. S. Eliot, 'Ash Wednesday', in *The Wasteland and Other Poems* (London, Faber, 1971).

5. Ch. LVIII of the Rule states, 'The one who is to be accepted into the community must promise . . . stability, conversion of life and obedience'; while ch. I roundly condemns monks termed 'wanderers' as 'always roving and never settling, they follow their own wills, enslaved by the attractions of gluttony.' *The Rule of St Benedict*, trans. Abbot Parry OSB (Leominster, Gracewing, 1990).

6. Adrian Hastings, 'Between Augustine and Columba', in Simon Barrow and Graeme Smith (eds), *Christian Mission in Western Society* (Churches Together in Britain and Ireland, 2001).

7. Quoted in a sermon by Eric James.

8. Vincent Donovan, *Christianity Rediscovered – An Epistle from the Masai* (London, SCM Press, 1982).

9. As Meister Eckhart articulated, 'Man's last and highest parting occurs when, for God's sake, he takes leave of God.' Sermon *Qui Audit Me*, quoted in Don Cupitt, *Taking Leave of God* (London, SCM Press, 1980), title page.

10. Julian of Norwich, ch. 22, *Revelations of Divine Love* (Harmondsworth, Penguin, 1966).

CD track list and credits

1. 'The cross in the 21st century' ('The Last Supper'*)
2. 'Father, forgive them; for they know not what they do' ('Kaddish for Bergen-Belsen'*)
3. 'Truly, I say to you, today you will be with me in Paradise' ('Burdens of Guilt'*)
4. 'Woman, behold, your son!. . . Behold, your mother!' ('Eva's Song')
5. 'Eli, Eli, lama sabachthani?. . . My God, my God, why hast thou forsaken me?' ('Credo')
6. 'I thirst' ('They Shall be Comforted'**)
7. 'It is finished' ('Golgotha'*)
8. 'Father, into thy hands I commit my spirit!' ('Within Me'**)

Titles in brackets refer to original recorded versions to be found on Adrian's CDs *Solo** and *Father***. The recordings of 'Credo' and 'Eva's Song' are previously unreleased.

All music composed by Adrian Snell.

Adrian Snell: piano; vocal on 'Credo'; guitar on 'Within Me'.
Hannah Alkire: cello.
Luca Genta: cello on 'They Shall be Comforted'; cello and soprano recorder on 'Within Me'.
Julian Gregory: violins on 'Within Me'.
Gill Balmain: oboe on 'Within Me'.
The Wellspring String Ensemble: strings on 'Eva's Song'.
String arrangement by Alex Robertson.

Hannah Alkire's cellos recorded at Absolute Sound Recording, Bethoud, Colorado, by Joe Scott.
Creative Development: Edmund Newell and Adrian Snell.
Additional production and CD mastering by Jonathan Lane.

Music published by Serious Music UK Ltd.

www.adrian-snell.com